A LOVE WORTH HAVING

Finding Unconditional Love
When Storms Arise

Temilolu Adegboye
&
Susannah Yetunde Oziegbe

Copyright © 2021 Temilolu Adegboye & Susannah Yetunde Oziegbe

All Rights Reserved. No part of this book may be reproduced in any manner whatsoever, or stored in any information storage system, or transmitted in any form or by any means, electronic, mechanical, photocopying, recording, or otherwise, without the prior written consent of the publisher, except in the case of brief quotations with proper reference, embodied in articles and reviews.

Printed in the United Kingdom
ISBN: 978-1-3999-0469-8
Published by: Susannah Yetunde Oziegbe
Editorial Production: The Editor's Chair

Scripture quotations from The Authorized (King James) Version. Rights in the Authorized Version in the United Kingdom are vested in the Crown. Reproduced by permission of the Crown's patentee, Cambridge University Press

Scripture quotations taken from the (NASB®) New American Standard Bible®, Copyright © 2020 by The Lockman Foundation. Used by permission. All rights reserved. www.lockman.org

Scripture quotations marked (NIV) are taken from the Holy Bible, New International Version®, NIV®. Copyright © 1973, 1978, 1984, 2011 by Biblica, Inc.™ Used by permission of Zondervan. All rights reserved worldwide. www.zondervan.com The "NIV" and "New International Version" are trademarks registered in the United States Patent and Trademark Office by Biblica, Inc.™

Scripture quotations marked (AMP) are taken from the Amplified Bible, Copyright © 1954, 1958, 1962, 1964, 1965, 1987 by The Lockman Foundation. Used by permission.

Scripture quotations marked (NKJV) are taken from the New King James Version®. Copyright© 1982 by Thomas Nelson. Used by permission. All rights reserved.

Scripture quotations marked (NLT) are taken from the Holy Bible, New Living Translation, copyright ©1996, 2004, 2015 by Tyndale House Foundation. Used by permission of Tyndale House Publishers, Carol Stream, Illinois 60188. All rights reserved.

Scripture quotations marked (TPT) are from The Passion Translation®. Copyright© 2017, 2018 by Passion & Fire Ministries, Inc. Used by permission. All rights reserved. ThePassionTranslation.com.

CONTENTS

Dedication *1*

Acknowledgements *2*

Foreword *5*

INTRODUCTION 8

CHAPTER ONE: The Beginning 9

CHAPTER TWO: New Year, New Me 17

CHAPTER THREE: The Journey 34

CHAPTER FOUR: Road To Recovery 46

CHAPTER FIVE: Support Systems 64

CHAPTER SIX: Dealing With Unexpected News 71

CHAPTER SEVEN: God's Master Plan 76

CHAPTER EIGHT: Unconditional Love 81

CHAPTER NINE: Finishing Strong 89

Picture Gallery *97*

Further Information *101*

About the Authors *102*

DEDICATION

This book is dedicated to our Lord and Saviour Jesus Christ who paid the ultimate sacrifice for us, and to all those who are battling cancer or who have lost a loved one to cancer. Keep fighting. Don't give up.

ACKNOWLEDGEMENTS

Temi could not write this section herself but her words were taken from a post she made on November 10th, 2016, as BabyTinks on Breastcancer.org. She wrote:

'First of all, I thank God for keeping me alive.

'My caregiver was my father during my treatment in India. My step mum couldn't go with me as she was having a high-risk pregnancy at the time. Since I had lost my mum to cancer, it fell on Dad to be my caregiver. He had his moments of fear, but he never allowed me to see them. My dad is my hero. I watched him stand by my side, worry while I was in the theatre, sit by my side during my chemo sessions, take me to the washroom, cook for me, force me to try to eat, give me my drugs, pray me to sleep, pray with me. He gave his all to me. When I think back on all the trouble he had to go through being my caregiver, I usually have tears in my eyes. He was super-amazing! Today, I thank him especially for the love and the care and the encouragement.

'My family members were amazing as well, especially my elder sister who was having her own cancer treatment at the same time as me. She was my support system. Sisters in the fight. We rock! We conquered.

'Mercy, my dear friend. You shocked me amongst all of my friends. You checked on me every day for the period of my treatment. You knew my treatment schedule as well as I knew it, my chemo days, my test days, my immune booster days, my every moment. You are the definition of true friendship. Love you, Girl.

'To every other fighter, don't relent in the fight. We are all conquerors. Champions. Fighters. Survivors. Don't give up. Don't lose hope. Together we can!'

Although Temi has gone to be with the Lord, her acknowledgements are still valid. For those who gave in cash and kindness towards Temi's care, we are grateful and pray that the Lord will reward you richly. Those who stood with us, prayed with us and supported us in our time of grief are too numerous to mention, but God knows you all. We love and appreciate you.

Thank you, Daniel, Ese and Uyi. You have journeyed with me through my own battles. Your support and encouragement as I worked to finish this book mean the world to me.

Thank you, Anu, for being there till the end and for holding Temi's hands as she went to be with our Lord. You are everything a person could ask for in a sister. Thank you, Banke and Wale, who though far away were never too busy and were always there to support Temi as she journeyed through her illness. Thank you, Halima and Bolu, for your care. And to our step mum, 'Mama', thank you for being there in every way.

Thank you, Eugene, for your love and support whilst Temi was in India. You were her knight in shining armour. You were an angel, whom God brought into her life when we could not be with her. You gave her joy and helped her enjoy the last few months of her life.

To the doctors and oncologists who took care of Temi in Nigeria and India, we are truly grateful. Specific thanks to Dr Ushie, Professor Ugwu, Dr Singh, Dr Das, Dr Ruquaya, Professor Emmanuel Agaba and Professor (Mrs) Patricia Agaba who all made treatment recommendations and referrals, and made every effort to ensure that Temi had the best possible care and was comfortable. Your emotional support was timely and greatly appreciated.

Thank you, Dad and Anu, for contributing to the words in this book to ensure we finished it. Thank you, Marjie, for your wonderful work of proofreading and your input. You did not know Temi but you got to meet her through her words. Uncle Femi, thank you for everything. You knew that Temi had started writing and you wished it could be published. Thank you Denise and your wonderful team of editors. I appreciate your valuable insight and contributions.

Thank you to everyone. God bless and keep you all.

FOREWORD

This is a love story candidly told, not by dying lips, but by a living soul. It is a story about a battle of faith. It's a story of how cancer died and Temi lives—in the hearts of her loved ones. It is a story of one little girl whose Great Father bid her come home before cancer could conclude its vilest act.

I remember preaching at Temi's celebratory funeral service of songs. I reminded everyone there of the paradox of living and dying. To celebrate a very short life is paradoxical, especially a life that had been shorter than most of those in that service and much shorter than we would have wished. Yet, we did!

When Temi was initially diagnosed, the first thing I noticed in her was understandably some mixed signals: a noticeable concern, and an acceptance of the reality, yet without resigning to fate. It wasn't a denial when she voiced rejection of that medical prognosis. Recalling her mum's case, I was disturbed. I leaned over to ask her father the local doctor's conclusion. "Breast cancer confirmed," he said. I turned to Temi again and blurted, "No matter what happens, we will have the last laugh, since there is nothing new God is trying to discover that He would use any of us for an experiment." Those were the words Temi and I shared so often till her last breath when she mocked cancer and exited her weary body.

In this book, you will read the story of Temi who believed in God every inch of the way. The battle was fierce, and Temi was dogged. Drugs were faithfully taken, as prescribed. Food, exercise, even sleeping regimens; some so uncomfortable and so unnatural to a particularly lively and boisterous young woman like Temi, were introduced, and judiciously followed. She did whatever was necessary.

Following her second treatment trip to India when the metastasised cancerous cells had spread to her lungs, liver and bones, some fear, doubt and dread spread through her spirit. But her confidence in God was unshaken. So, in some ways, this book is a story of moments of fear, instances of dread, and some bouts of doubt. Temi wasn't in dread of death, nor was she seized by bouts of doubt in God. No, it was the sovereignty of God and His unquestionable love that were the only dread.

This story in this book comes in two blended parts. The first part is told by Temi in her own words and the latter has been beautifully scripted by her sister, Yetunde (Susannah), as a family account of all that took place while the battle raged. This book is a story of a daughter of faith who became a preacher of faith in the days of pain. Though our outward man decays, our inner man prevails. When we talked about this book with Temi, she wanted to publish it as a testimonial post-cancer treatment. We talked about some titles. Some writing ideas and even likely book layouts were considered.

I am glad that the family asked me to write this foreword, just as I was called to speak at the funeral service of songs. Temi's story has been told with such intentionality—firstly to honour God; secondly to celebrate the Author of life who gives us life so generously, and thirdly to inspire hope among those who may be boxed into a corner by debilitating illness like cancer. I hope you find these three themes in this work.

One day I asked Temi to tell me what was happening inside her. "Uncle, you know me now. The way things are now, I am more alive than in the days before the discovery of this ugly visitor." That was the truth she powerfully expressed that evening. I remember telling guests at her funeral to note the contradiction of life and death—life does not permit full human control; death does not follow logic or operate chronologically, and despite death, we will live forever!

I hope reading this book helps you to see life through death, to choose joy amid sadness, to anticipate divine pleasure in the terrain of pain. Temi's cancer story is told the best way people living for eternity could explain the illogicality we all face as mere mortals.

Canon Timothy Olonade
El-Rehoboth Global Missions
Jos, Nigeria 08037865130
March 31st, 2021

INTRODUCTION

On Thursday 20th September 1984, a star was born; a light came on. Oh, the eyes that lit up every room! Temilolu Adegboye (popularly called 'Temi') was born into the family of Rev. David Adekunle Adegboye and the late Mrs Folashayo Oluyinka Adegboye.

My sister Temi was loved by all who knew her. She made friends easily and was always the life of the party. Everyone wanted to be around her. As a young child, she was nicknamed 'Atupa Parlour' (lantern of the living room), which was appropriate because there was always a light in her eyes that endeared her to everyone she knew.

Towards the end of 2015, when she was just 31 years old, she received the diagnosis no one wants to hear. Despite this, Temi was a true warrior, a fighter, a trooper. She remained positive throughout her two-year battle with cancer. Even through all the pain and difficult days, she maintained her unique smile and light in her eyes. Nothing seemed to faze her.

Temi was a determined young lady who loved the Lord fervently and served Him faithfully till the end. She held on to hope and encouraged others around her to be strong. She never doubted that God would perform the ultimate miracle of complete healing which He alone can do. Our joy and consolation are that she is in Heaven now, pain-free, cancer-free, with a new and glorified body that can know no decay.

Temi wanted to share her experience with the world. This is a story she started writing and I finished for her. This is not just another cancer patient's experience but is also a story about God's faithfulness. It's a story about how God shows His love for His children in seasons of pain and how He journeys with them. It also includes the stories and verses from scripture she drew strength from, and the revelations that built her faith in God.

This is a story about Temi's victory over cancer. This is a story about *A Love Worth Having*.

Chapter ONE

THE BEGINNING

Fear gripped me when I noticed the lump in my left breast one morning while I was getting dressed for work. It was quite strange because I have always been a hypochondriac. I was someone who always went for my health checks regularly and had my blood tested often; not because I was expecting to find anything wrong, but because that's just who I am. My stomach felt as if it had flipped over because of what I had just felt. I told Anu, my younger sister, who was also getting dressed for work, about the lump I had found and she advised me to have it checked out at the hospital.

I went to the hospital two days later and the doctor suggested that I should have a scan, which I did. Unfortunately, the sonographer said, 'Ma'am, there's nothing to worry about and there's nothing to fear. The scan shows that the lumps are non-cancerous but I would advise you to come back in three months to do another scan.'

I gave a sigh of relief. My mind had conjured up so many dark things as I had lain there having the scan, so on hearing those words, I whispered a prayer of thanks to God that it wasn't bad news.

Life went on for me as usual—work, church, home. My routine was exhausting. I was working as a project advisor for a loan company. I had little or no time for myself for personal development because my job at the time was so demanding. I had informed my parents about the lump I'd discovered, the visit to the hospital, the outcome and the date of my next doctor's appointment. They were a bit disturbed but I assured them that I was totally okay. Their fear was because at the time I'd discovered the lump, Yetunde, my eldest sister in the United Kingdom was in hospital following surgery for ovarian cancer. I understand how any parent would be worried and disturbed;

I mean, who wouldn't be? None of this seemed to scare me any longer because I had found solace in 2 Timothy 1:7

> *'For God has not given us a spirit of fear, but of power and of love and of a sound mind.' (NKJV)*

As a single girl, I loved to spend Christmas at my parents' house. It was always a time to look forward to; so much to do, so much love, so much to eat and a special time for the family reunion. I had been looking forward to Christmas since the previous Christmas celebration! Little did I know there was much more than that lying in wait for me. But as the Bible says in 1 Thessalonians 5:18,

> *'In everything give thanks; for this is the will of God in Christ Jesus for you.' (NKJV)*

This may sound absurd, but whatever happens, it is the will of God in Christ Jesus for us. That doesn't mean God is wicked. He never makes mistakes and also never wants any of His children to suffer. Unaware of what was happening inside my body, I thanked God.

I arrived home for Christmas and one of the first things my parents talked about was the lump. I took my mama into another room and guided her hand so that she could feel the lump. All she said was 'okay', but the look on her face said otherwise. I assured her that there was nothing to worry about, just like the doctor had told me when I had gone for my scan. They had however arranged with Dr Ushie (our family doctor) to come around and check it out, obviously not convinced with the first doctor's opinion. That turned out to be a very wise decision.

> *'Wisdom is the principal thing; therefore, get wisdom. And in all your getting, get understanding.' (Proverbs 4:7 NKJV)*

Dr Ushie came, and after I'd told him the first doctor's conclusion, he decided to do a manual examination of the lump. After hearing what the previous doctor had said, he was furious and said, 'No one should ever treat a lump in the body with levity until it has been confirmed what type of lump it is.' He told me that I would have to go to the hospital for a biopsy to ascertain what type of lump it was. (A biopsy is an examination of tissue removed from a living body to discover the presence, cause, or extent of a disease and is usually done when a test suggests an area of tissue in the body isn't normal. It may be called an abnormality, a mass, a lump or a tumour, but it has to be biopsied.) My mind was greatly disturbed at the sound of all of this, but I remembered what Proverbs 3:5-6 says and I was consoled, even during that troubled moment.

> 'Trust in the Lord with all your heart, and lean not on your own understanding, in all your ways acknowledge Him, and He shall direct your path.' (NKJV)

When it seems like the tides are rising, take refuge in the One who created the waters. God is the only one Who can give peace amid chaos. Philippians 4:7 tells us

> 'And the peace of God, which surpasses all understanding will guard your hearts and minds through Christ Jesus.' (NKJV)

The fateful day arrived when they were going to take a sample to send for the biopsy. I was taken to the hospital. I am not one who likes hospitals (does anyone?!), but it was necessary. My younger sister told me not to worry as she was going to be waiting outside the theatre for me. It is so important to have the right set of people around you always; that's why the Bible tells us to watch what company we keep. The right kind of people are always a good source of encouragement when the tides are rising; people who strengthen and encourage you, who will lift you up no matter how deep it seems you have sunk.

> *'Do not be unequally yoked together with unbelievers. For what fellowship has righteousness with lawlessness? And what communication has light with darkness? And what accord has Christ with Belial? Or what part has a believer with an unbeliever? And what agreement has the temple of God with idols? For you are the temple of the Living God. As God has said; I will dwell and walk among them. I will be their God, and they shall be my people, therefore come out from among them and be separate, says the Lord. Do not touch what is unclean. And I will receive you, I will be a father to you and you shall be my sons and daughters, says the Lord Almighty.' (2 Corinthians 6:14-18 NKJV)*

Another striking section from the Bible that talks about the kind of people you should surround yourself with is Psalms 133:1-3

> *'Behold how good and how pleasant it is for brethren to dwell together in unity. It is like the precious oil upon the head running down on the beard, the beard of Aaron...*
>
> *...it is like the dew of Hermon, descending upon the mountains of Zion; for there the Lord commanded the blessing– Life forevermore.' (NKJV)*

Waiting for the doctor to be ready was frustrating; a seemingly endless wait. Finally, he was ready for me.

'This way please,' he said, as he motioned in the direction for me to go. 'You will need to change your clothes into the hospital dress as we're ready for you now.' I gladly changed, hugged my sister and went towards the theatre.

The theatre was very 'uninteresting' because all there was in it was a large light stand, the theatre table and some dishes holding sterilised instruments. The doctor was whistling a song from the famous Reggae musician, Bob Marley, 'Redemption Song'. I guess that was his way of calming down, but I'm not sure if it calmed me down or stressed me out even more! I just wanted the procedure to be over. I wasn't sure exactly what it was he was going to do to me. He finally came and looked at the area with the lump, then looked at me and told me not to worry because everything would be fine. He started to draw the letter 'C' with his fingers on the part closest to the lump—his way of making a rough map of his work area. Next, he put on his gloves and reached for a syringe that he had drawn the anaesthetic agent into. He gave me a jab around the work area that was intended to make the area numb. I remained calm. The words from Psalms 23:4 came to mind.

> *'Yea, though I walk through the valley of the shadow of death, I will fear no evil; for You are with me; Your rod and Your staff they comfort me.' (NKJV)*

The comfort the Holy Spirit gives cannot be over-emphasised. John 14:16 says,

> *'And I pray the Father and He shall give you another Comforter, that He may abide with you forever.' (NKJV)*

Jesus had good reason to ask the Father to send the Holy Spirit. He is our comforter, advocate, guide, intercessor, Spirit of truth, Spirit of God, witness and teacher. When we don't understand something, we can ask the Teacher. When we can't reach the Father, we can use the Intercessor. When we need counsel, we can ask the Advocate. He is everything we need in whatever circumstance we find ourselves. Listen carefully because He speaks in a still, small voice.

The doctor reached for the surgical blade and cut me at the point where he had mapped out earlier. 'Oh my God! What has he done?' I thought to myself. 'I thought he was just going to get a sample of the lump to send to the lab, but he has cut me up!' At that point, it hit me that this was actually a surgery. I felt blood trickle down my body, but there was no way I could say to him now, 'Stop, I don't want to do this!' I could feel and hear the tearing of my flesh, but somehow, I remained still.

> *'Be still and know that I am God. I will be exalted among the nations; I will be exalted in the earth. The Lord of Hosts is with us, the God of Jacob is our refuge.' (Psalm 46:10-11 NKJV)*

The thought that my heart might come out through the opening was what made me keep my mouth shut through the procedure. Ten minutes...

Twenty minutes ... Thirty minutes and then came a scream with me panting. That really hurt! It appeared that the effect of the anaesthetic had worn off and the doctor asked for another shot to be administered to me. Then there was some calm and quiet again. Forty-five minutes ... one hour and the procedure was still going on. It felt like forever but after about two and a half hours, it was finally over. I overheard the doctor saying to one of the assistants, 'We couldn't go any deeper; it's deep inside her muscle.' I kept wondering what he meant by that because I had already been sutured back up which meant that the lump was still inside me. But the Bible says in Matthew 6:27, 34

> *'Which of you by worrying can add one cubit to his stature ... therefore do not worry about tomorrow, for tomorrow will worry about its own things. Sufficient for the day is its own trouble.' (NKJV)*

My sister met me in the changing room where I had to change from the hospital dress back into my own clothes. She hugged me lightly as she knew that I had just undergone a procedure. She looked at me and said, 'T-Mama, I am so proud of you! You are such a strong woman and I admire your strength.' She meant those words, but my response was unexpected and out of character. 'Is that supposed to make me feel better?' I retorted. 'You lied to me, you lied to me, Baby Girl. You told me it wasn't going to take time and that it wouldn't hurt much.' And my tears started to flow. She told me that she hadn't lied to me. She simply hadn't known about the process in this particular hospital, as all hospitals have different means of collecting samples for biopsy.

We got home not long after, and I had to start with the drugs I'd been given at the hospital. The next few days passed in a blur because the year was almost over.

Chapter TWO

NEW YEAR, NEW ME

The New Year came and of course, the excitement was almost uncontrollable. We were all excited to be alive to see the New Year. It came time for our regular 'New Year, new me' story and New Year resolutions. I honestly just wanted the year to draw me closer to God, to fulfil my purpose and calling more than I had done the previous year and to have an outstanding walk and relationship with Him.

I had butterflies in my stomach. I didn't know what the new year had in store for me, but I was optimistic that I would attract and get only the best of the year for me and mine... but then thoughts of my as yet unknown biopsy test results kept flashing through my mind every other minute. Somehow, however, I found assurance in God as I knew His plans for me were for good and not for evil, to bring me to an expected end. (Jeremiah 29:11)

It felt like an endless wait. So many things kept running through my mind. I really didn't know what to expect, but I kept my focus on God and also kept my mind positive and on positive things. It was the 4th January when we received a call from the laboratory informing us that the test result was ready. I was feeling a mixture of emotions. Part of me was happy that the test result was finally ready, but the other part was scared because I didn't know what to expect. But I never thought of the worst, I didn't entertain any negative thoughts. The wait was over, but what to expect was another thing.

The eagerness to know the result made me rush to collect it and take it to the doctor. The very curious part of me opened the unsealed envelope containing the result. God knows I read all through it but I didn't see anything worrying in it. We can consciously choose to see what we want to see. In the face of negativity, choose to see the positive. Now, that doesn't mean that you should close your eyes to what is reality, but it's a choice.

After waiting for what felt like forever, he finally showed up and ushered me into a secluded office. The office had stacks of books in it, the table at the end was terribly dusty and a stale smell filled the air. The room looked like a place where the board of directors of a company or organisation would hold their meetings. *What is so serious as to bring me in here?* I thought to myself... *well, I am here doctor, let me hear you.* 'You are welcome here once again,' the doctor said, smiling. *What is this doctor talking about?* I wondered.

Can you just interpret this result and leave the pleasantries out of it? I was tempted to say this but restrained myself from talking.

The build-up of suspense was already making my blood pressure rise—I could feel it.

I wasn't relaxed at all. 'What do you understand about lumps in the body?' The doctor's question broke my thoughts. His voice sounded so loud to me that I jumped. I answered, 'A lump is an unwanted growth that shouldn't be in the body'. He said that he wanted to ascertain how much I knew about the condition and then calmly said to me in these exact words, 'Well, Madam Temi, the lumps are not non-cancerous.' This meant that the lumps that I had discovered were cancerous. CANCER??? WHAT??? HOW COULD IT BE??? HOW IS THAT EVEN POSSIBLE??? The questions seemed endless in my head. 'The result showed it was Stage 3.' He continued talking, but I could only see his lips moving. I didn't hear a word of what he was saying. I really didn't know what to think at all. It seemed as though I was having a nightmare and all I needed to do was just wake up. Unfortunately, this was far from being a nightmare.

At this point, I would like to pause to say that it is part of human nature to react this way. As humans, we tend to want to ask questions and wonder why. However, what matters is to realise that there's a Higher Power involved. Let's examine this by looking critically at the story of Job in the Bible.

Job was described by God as a man who was blameless and upright, who feared God and shunned evil. We would think that nothing could affect him because he was very wealthy and because God had described him in such glowing terms. He had it all but when he least expected it, tragedy hit him like a tsunami. All his possessions—seven thousand sheep, three thousand camels, five hundred yoke of oxen, five hundred female donkeys, a very large household—gone. Everything was gone. He received such bad news. And the devil being who he is said that Job would curse God to His face because of the calamity that had befallen him. Job's human nature emerged after hearing about the loss of all his possessions—'... *Job arose, tore his robe and shaved his head...' (Job 1:20 NKJV)*. In this, Job didn't sin, even though his grief was great.

God is not a wicked God. I want to establish that fact. He says that His thoughts about us are of good and not of evil. God allows certain things to happen for a specific reason. There are several instances in the Bible where God allowed difficult things to happen and all of them were for God's glory to be seen. God never makes mistakes, so whenever any form of calamity or tragedy hits us, we should trust Him. God didn't promise us a temptation-free or trouble-free life. He promised that He wouldn't leave us. He promised that even when trials came, He wouldn't give us a temptation that was too much for us to bear.

> *'No temptation has overtaken you except such as is common to man; but God is faithful, Who will not allow you to be tempted beyond what you are able, but with the temptation will also make the way of escape, that you may be able to bear it.' (1 Corinthians 10:13 NKJV)*

I heard the doctor's last words. 'It's not a death sentence, life can still go on for you, just a few changes, but you will definitely survive this. A treatment plan will be drawn up and communicated to you in the shortest space of time, as we have to commence treatment as soon as possible.'

I thanked him, said my goodbyes and stood up to leave the boardroom. As I walked through the long walkway leading to the hospital's exit, a certain fear gripped me. Many thoughts went through my head. My whole life flashed through my eyes in split seconds. I thought to myself, *This is the same cancer that killed my mother; here I am diagnosed with Stage-3 breast cancer at the age of 31, unmarried,* amongst other thoughts. I had to shut those thoughts out. I had to remind myself that it wasn't the end for me. I literally picked myself up from the floor, dusted myself down and encouraged myself to be strong while also accepting the truth. Yes, life isn't fair, but God is. He heals the broken-hearted, the bruised and the wounded. Sometimes we do not understand why certain things happen to us the way they do, but we know God and we should learn to trust Him.

> *'He gives power to the weak, and to those who have no might He increases strength. Even the youths shall faint and be weary, and the young men shall utterly fall, but those who wait on the Lord shall renew their strength; they shall mount up with wings like eagles, they shall run and not be weary, they shall walk and not faint.' (Isaiah 40:29-31 NKJV)*

In whatever situation we find ourselves, God always has a way of reassuring us with His Word.

FAMILY REACTION

I arrived home looking like a chicken that had been soaked in water. After I'd told everyone what the doctor had said, there was so much love from them all. I felt supported and I hadn't even started the treatment yet. My dad wasn't home at the time, but eventually arrived back and was told the bad news. He was quite moved upon hearing the news of my diagnosis but he knew he had to be strong for me as I was looking to him for strength. He asked me to sit down right in front of him and he held my hands and told me something that I wouldn't forget in a long while. He told me of a time years ago, when I wasn't even born yet and my mum had been faced with a challenge. They'd been in London at the time. He'd thought he was going to lose her when she was rushed to hospital and he'd had to sign the consent form for her to be operated on. He said that the pain he'd gone through had been nothing compared to what she'd been going through. He told me that my mum had been a very strong woman even up until her death, which had happened more than thirty-five years after that incident. He told me, 'I know this is hard for you right now. I cannot say that I know exactly how you feel or what is going on in your head but I want you to put on the fighter's spirit. I need you to fight this. Do you see how your sister has had to fight all this while? I need you to be strong and you have to be bold and you have to survive. I do not want to lose you; I will not lose you—God will see you through this process.'

My sister had been diagnosed with ovarian cancer the previous year and it had been quite a battle for her but she was fighting to stay alive with all of God's help. My dad then took me to a portion of the Bible that says,

> 'So you shall serve the Lord your God, and He will bless your bread and your water. And I will take sickness away from the midst of you. No one shall suffer miscarriage or be barren in your land; I will fulfil the number of your days.' (Exodus 23:25-26 NKJV)

After hearing all those words from my father, I felt like a soldier on the battlefront, even though I was unaware of what the battle in front of me looked like.

My mama too had a moment with me just to strengthen me and to encourage me. She was pregnant at the time and told me that when she'd encountered such a trying time, felt that she was going to lose her pregnancy, and all she was seeing was blood, that God had taken her to a portion of the Bible and she had drawn inspiration and assurance from there.

> *'Jesus said to her, I am the resurrection and the life. He who believes in me, though he may die, he shall live. And whoever lives and believes in Me shall never die. Do you believe this?' (John 11:25-26 NKJV)*

She told me how that scripture had ministered to her and that she believed Jesus is the resurrection and the life. Jesus is life. So, whoever believes in Him shall live. She'd spoken life into her unborn baby. She encouraged me so much with that scripture.

When I had retired to my room that night and was doing my devotion before I slept, I went to that same Bible passage and I asked God to give me my own assurance. I wanted Him to give me something to hold onto. I wanted my own revelation because the Bible says that we shall work out our own salvation with fear and trembling. God took me to the story of Lazarus which happens to also be in John 11. But God took me to verse 4, Jesus' response when he heard about the illness of Lazarus.

> *'When Jesus heard that, He said, "This sickness is not unto death, but for the glory of God, that the Son of God may be glorified through it."' (NKJV)*

Jesus didn't go immediately to meet with Lazarus after Mary sent word to Him about her brother's illness but He waited where He was for two more days before heading to Judea with His disciples.

That was all I needed, and God gave it to me. With this scripture in hand, I felt I could conquer the world. God is an awesome God. He knows how to comfort us in our times of distress.

WHAT NEXT?

We had to think fast about possible solutions. My parents did a lot of reading and a lot of research. From their research, they realised that some studies showed that cancer cells cannot thrive in a highly alkalised environment, but they thrive very well in an acidic environment. That isn't to say that the body doesn't need acid, a healthy body needs 80 per cent alkaline and 20 per cent acid to function properly. So, one of the major things we had to do was to work on changing my diet and raising my level of alkalinity. Honestly, it wasn't the easiest of tasks to do, but I didn't have much of a choice. And it turned out to be not so bad after all.

My meals comprised of vegetables (a whole lot of vegetables!), fruits, brown rice, and whole-wheat bread. I didn't eat anything that was processed. NO SUGAR. Yes! NO SUGAR. Sea salt, extra virgin olive oil, carrots, cucumber, lettuce, scaly fish, garlic. NO SODA.

THE APPOINTMENT WITH THE DOCTOR

Doctor Ushie, who has been our family doctor for as long as I can remember, referred me to another doctor, Professor Benjamin Ugwu, because Dr Ushie had to go to a medical outreach in another state within Nigeria.

At first, getting an appointment to see the professor felt like a Herculean task. Finally, after three failed attempts, I was able to see him. I was there with my daddy. The professor examined me and laid the options out on the table for us. He advised that I be sent to India and said that he would give me the available options and then I should pick which worked best for me or was most convenient for me. The first option was to refer me to a hospital in India where one area of specialisation was oncology (the treatment of cancer) and where they could do a breast conservation surgery for me. The second option was for me to have a mastectomy in Nigeria. A mastectomy is the total removal of the breast.

After hearing the two options laid out for me, I couldn't even do the thinking on my own. This was quite a tough decision to make and I had to get my family involved in the process.

Trying to work everything out clouded my mind. I was troubled because I knew that directly or indirectly, whatever decision we would take would affect us one way or the other. Despite the situation and the troubled state of my mind, I kept myself at rest because I knew Who held my life.

> *'For you died, and your life is hidden with Christ in God.' (Colossians 3:3 NKJV)*

The thoughts that came to my mind were the costs that would be involved in going to India for surgery and treatment and, if I had to be in Nigeria, what was going to happen?

But God surely works in mysterious ways. We were able to get a quotation from the hospital in India. The estimate was scary, but we knew that God would provide a means for us to be able to go.

While we were trying to raise the funds for me to go to India, the professor advised me to have certain tests carried out. He requested a CT scan of my chest and abdomen. I was also asked to have an x-ray done. All of this was to make sure there was no spread of the disease to any other part of the body. Thankfully, there was none. God is awesome.

The professor advised that I should be given one cycle of chemotherapy in Nigeria before going to India to help to keep the disease contained in one place so it didn't spread. Chemotherapy drugs interfere with cancer cells' ability to divide and reproduce. The hospital ran all the other necessary tests to make sure my body was well enough to have the first cycle of chemotherapy. These included liver function, kidney function and full blood count. These tests were needed to assess my body's health, as well as to ensure that I would be able to cope with the possible side effects. For example, blood tests can detect liver problems which could mean that a particular chemotherapy would be unsuitable. Chemotherapy drugs are also referred to as cytotoxic agents which are not only toxic to cancerous cells but also have the potential to damage normal cells. They are metabolised (broken down) in the liver, which could be harmed if it wasn't working properly. Also, the blood counts needed to be checked, because the treatment would reduce the number of red and white blood cells as well as the platelets. If the blood counts were low, the doctors might delay treatment.

On 25th January 2016 I had my first cycle of chemotherapy. I wouldn't say that it was a pleasant experience. Initially, I had no idea exactly what chemotherapy was. I used to think it was a machine type of treatment. We got to the hospital and we were given a prescription to go and get the drugs. After that, I was admitted. The professor had an emergency case to attend to, so he had referred me to another doctor. That doctor eventually asked another doctor to administer the chemotherapy to me.

Chemotherapy (called 'chemo' for short) is a drug given through the vein; it is a systemic treatment meaning that the drug flows through the bloodstream to nearly every part of the body. The chemotherapy was administered to me and I was later discharged.

The next day I felt very sick. It seemed as though I'd been okay until that chemo was administered to me. I hadn't been warned about the sickness that comes as a side effect of chemotherapy so I was shocked when I started vomiting uncontrollably. I found out later that chemotherapy has several side effects which include nausea and vomiting, alopecia (hair loss), fatigue, hearing impairment, and neutropenia (low white blood cell count). This weakens the immune system, making the body more susceptible to infections. Chemo also causes thrombocytopenia (low blood platelet counts that can cause blood clotting problems), anaemia, mouth inflammation and ulcers, loss of appetite, dry skin and nails, diarrhoea or constipation and depression. That's quite a list and some people experience other effects but I won't list them all. You get the idea!

I wasn't experiencing all of these side effects yet, as this was just the first cycle I'd had. An anti-nausea drug is usually given to help reduce the sickness that comes with chemo, but, unfortunately, I wasn't given that. When the vomiting became too much and we realised that there was nothing left in my system and I was unable to eat, we had to call the doctor my professor had handed me over to. He had given us his number and said we should call him if there were any issues at all, so we did. He told us of a medicine that we should get which I should take thirty minutes before eating.

Something else happened that day. I made a resolve in my heart that I was going to use everything there was in me to fight this cancer. I will tell you what led to this decision. One of the times when I rushed from the room where I was lying to the bathroom to go and vomit, I was in such a hurry that I forgot to close the door. My dad rushed in to come and help me. I was standing with my head over the toilet bowl and my dad was rubbing my back for me. When he noticed I had stopped vomiting, he brought me some water to wash my face and to rinse my mouth. Afterwards, I turned around and was going to leave the bathroom. My dad put out his hand for me to use as support. When I placed my hands in his, I noticed that my dad's hands were shaking. I had never seen my dad scared in my life. He has always been a very brave man. But that day, I felt his fear and said in my heart, *God, please keep me alive for this man who has always been my support and who has always shown me what bravery is.*

The next couple of days after my chemo weren't fun at all. I am a light-skinned person by nature, but I noticed that now I had turned very dark. I looked like a corpse that had been in a morgue for the past ten days and I hardly recognised myself. Once again, I didn't understand what was happening to me. I became very emotional and cranky but I had to pretend that everything was okay because I didn't want my dad to become overly worried. Sometimes when he knocked on my door before coming into the room (he had a particular way of knocking so you would know it was him at the door), I would quickly put a smile on my face. When he'd ask me if I was okay, I would tell him with a smile that I doing fine. However, deep down inside I knew that something wasn't right. Despite this, I kept my trust in God throughout the experience. He is a gracious God and His grace always abounds for us. It is better to trust in God than in anything man can do.

> *'Blessed is the man who trusts in the Lord, whose hope is in the Lord. For he shall be like a tree planted by the waters, which spreads out its roots by the river, and will not fear when heat comes; but its leaf will be green, and will not be anxious in the year of drought, nor will cease from yielding fruits.' (Jeremiah 17:7-8 NKJV)*

Sometimes God takes us through the fire, not to burn us, but to teach us to trust Him completely. The word trust is a big word. The whole of life is about trust. Trust, as defined by Webster's dictionary, is the belief that someone or something is reliable, good, honest and effective. This trust to which I refer is a TOTAL RELIANCE on God.

> *'When you pass through the waters, I will be with you; and through the rivers, they shall not overflow you. When you walk through the fire, you shall not be burned, nor shall the flame scorch you. For I Am the Lord your God, the Holy One of Israel, your saviour; I gave Egypt for your ransom, Ethiopia and Seba in your place.' (Isaiah 43:2-3 NKJV)*

God wants us to be totally dependent on Him and we should learn to trust in His ways and His will. He never makes mistakes. God isn't a wicked God. He never wants any of us to suffer and He knows all the pain we feel. At the same time though, He chooses who or what or how He wants to show His glory. God wants us to prosper as our souls prosper and, above all, He wants us to be in good health. So, it's not as if God gave me cancer; it's not as if He doesn't love me. He has chosen to show His glory in this way. He wants me to rely on Him fully and to trust Him that as I pass through this 'fire' called cancer, it will not burn me.

Gold in its natural state does not appeal to the eyes. For it to be pure gold, it has to pass through the fire. It has to be burnt and baked. When things happen to us that we don't understand, we should see them as part of the refining process. Just as gold has to be refined, we like gold need to be purified.

The hospital in India sent us an estimate and a proforma invoice telling us how much my treatment there was going to cost. I told God that this battle was His battle and I was going to let Him fight it for me. The figure on the proforma invoice was scary because I knew I didn't have that amount of money and neither did my family. It was a real test of our faith and trust in God. I didn't let the figure scare me, however, because I had my trust in the One who owns the gold, the silver and the world's most priceless jewels. The One who owns the cattle on a thousand hills; the One who is a giver and a generous God.

When we take God for Who He is, He will be to us as we see Him. We realise that HE IS ENOUGH for everything we need. He can displace another person just to place you. He is the God who breaks protocols for His children. Oh yes! For everything, God is. When God told Moses to go to Pharaoh to tell him to let the children of Israel go (Exodus 3), Moses asked God, 'Who do I say sent me?'

> 'And God said to Moses, "I AM WHO I AM." And He said, "Thus you shall say to the children of Israel, 'I AM has sent me to you.'"' (Exodus 3:14 NKJV)

God is I AM. Whatever our perception of Him, that He will be to us. However we see Him, He says, 'I AM'. I AM your healer. I AM your deliverer. I AM your saviour. I AM your ever-exceeding joy. I AM your everything. It is important to note here that we should never ever undermine or underestimate Who God is. I knew God was able to do exceedingly abundantly above all I could ask or think, so my faith wasn't shaken.

The hospital said that they were expecting me already. We had barely two weeks to raise the huge sum of money but I knew God was going to come to our rescue and He would raise up helpers for me.

It was such an emotional time for me. God used many outstanding people to make my trip to India possible. People I have never met in my life came through for me and some donations just made me cry. I couldn't have been happier to have identified with everyone who gave and donated. What better way to be loved? This is the true meaning of 'A LOVE WORTH HAVING'. I am so thankful to everyone God used to provide for me. I wept when I heard that someone had given a thousand naira. Now, it's not the quantity, but the heart behind giving. This is an example of how much the Father loves us, that He gave. He gave generously to us.

> 'For God so loved the world that He gave His only begotten son, that whoever believes in Him should not perish but have everlasting life.' (John 3:16 NKJV)

God teaches us how to give by the demonstration of love that He gave. He could have given an angel, a sheep, or someone else, but He gave His only begotten son. That is A LOVE WORTH HAVING.

God uses what we give Him as a measure to bless us and give back to us. Regardless of how much or how little we give to Him, the emphasis is on the word 'give'. The Samaritan woman (John chapter 4) was asked by Jesus to GIVE Him a drink and she answered, 'Jews have no dealing with Samaritans'. But Jesus answered and said to her,

> *'If you knew the gift of God and Who it is who says to you "give me a drink," you would have asked Him and He would have given you living water'. (John 4:10 NKJV)*

We aren't always going to be asked to give, but whenever we have an opportunity to give, let's give. It may be the Father using a situation to teach you to give. When we have needs, God, who is in Heaven, doesn't physically come down and knock on our doors to give to us; He uses people to meet our needs. He gives to us from the abundance of the earth. As it is, all the people who gave to me answered the Master's call.

> *"For I was hungry and you gave me something to eat, I was thirsty and you gave me something to drink, I was a stranger and you invited me in, I needed clothes and you clothed me, I was sick and you looked after me, I was in prison and you came to visit me." Then the righteous will answer him, "Lord, when did we see you hungry and feed you, or thirsty and give you something to drink? When did we see you a stranger and invite you in, or needing clothes and clothe you? When did we see you sick or in prison and go to visit you?" The King will reply, "I tell you the truth, whatever you did for one of the least of these brothers of mine, you did for me."' (Matthew 25:35-40 NIV)*

When you give to the Lord, He gives it back to you a thousand-fold.

> *'Give, and it will be given to you, good measure, pressed down, shaken together, and running over will be put into your bosom. For with the same measure that you use, it shall be measured back to you.' (Luke 6:38 NKJV)*

God used everyone who donated to help me and I am sure without any doubt that God will give back to them all.

It was a bit strange when I approached some people to ask them for help—people I know could afford to sponsor my treatment—but was turned down. I learned many lessons from the process. It taught me that 'the arm of flesh shall fail you'. Our focus should be on God and not on our connections or who we think has it all, because it is only God who has it all.

MY HAIR STARTED TO FALL OUT! I cried so hard when I noticed it. I had just braided my hair three weeks before. My full head of hair had been an asset that others, including my sisters, had admired about me and now it was falling out. I had known that it was a possibility but still I was not prepared when it happened. At one point later, all I could feel on my head was skin. My youngest sister empathised when I cried. She said that she was going to cut her hair as well to make me feel better, but I told her not to. I sent my eldest sister a text saying, 'My hair is falling out.' Even though she was far away, she said that she wished she could hug me right then. This made me feel better. She asked if I had a wig and I said that I did not. I made up my mind then that I would loosen my braids and maybe cut the remaining hair and just rock the low-cut like that. I planned to get a wig too, just in case.

So, I decided to cut my hair and my dad thought it would be less traumatising if I cut the first few strands myself. I got a pair of scissors and cut out a few strands of braids even though it hurt my heart to do this. My sister helped cut off the remainder. Dad walked with me to the salon close to the house to get a tidier look. I'll admit I did not look too bad, and at least I wasn't completely bald.

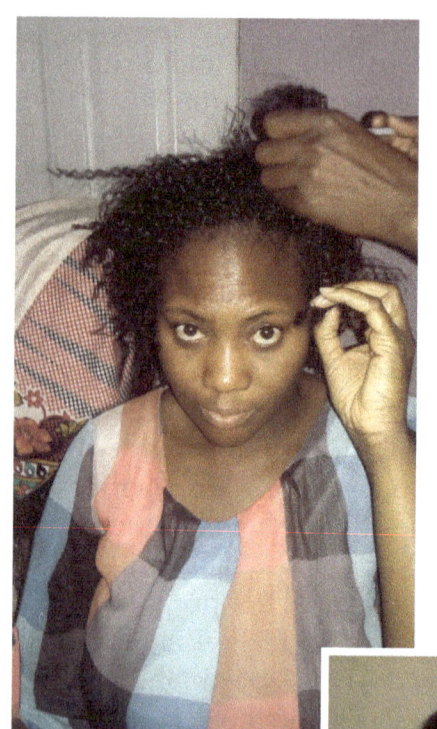
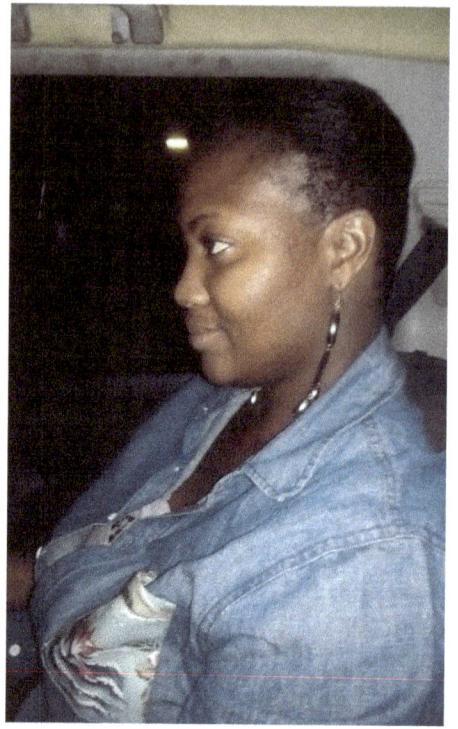

Chapter THREE

THE JOURNEY

Everything was put in place for my trip to India. My dad was going with me, as the professor had advised because a father figure would be needed when we got to India.

Our visa interview was scheduled for the fifth of February. We drove from Jos to Abuja where the Indian Embassy is located. It wasn't such a long drive, but for me, it felt like one. I just wanted everything to be over. I wanted to fast forward to the time when I knew this whole process would be done. Different thoughts kept coming to my mind. The devil kept telling me that the road we were driving on would be the last time I would ever be on that road. He kept saying evil things to me, things like I wouldn't see my family again after I had said goodbye to them but I stood my ground on the word of God. I reminded the devil of the words God had given me and God's promise of good health. I kept confessing positive things and we got to Abuja safely.

The next morning, we were up early and went to the Indian Embassy. There were so many people there, everyone with their own problem. We were eventually called in after about two and a half hours of waiting. We had all the requirements with us. We were attended to by a very disinterested-looking man. He was on the phone for half the time talking in Hindi. He motioned me to sit down. He collected my international passport and signalled that I should put my fingers on the machine to get my fingerprints, all the while talking on the phone. He took my data page, asked me to stand up and my dad to sit down so he could also get his biodata. He eventually got off the phone and asked us to come back in a week to collect the visa. Ah! A week? That seemed too long to wait. Dad spoke to him calmly and asked, 'Sir, please, isn't there a way we can get it earlier than that?' The man replied, "Okay, come back in five days and collect your visas by 4 pm.' That was it. That was how easy it was for us to get our visas. There was still a slight problem though. The day we were supposed to get our visas was the day we had booked our tickets to leave Nigeria for India. We just asked God to take control of everything.

We collected our passports and visas just in time and made it to the airport on time as well!

It was a very long trip. We first flew to Dubai then caught a connecting flight to Delhi. When we arrived at Delhi International Airport, we saw someone holding up a card that had my name on it. Oh wow! The hospital had sent for me to be picked up. That made me feel special.

The trip was a very different experience from any I'd had before. The closest I had been to India before now was *Zee World* (an Indian channel on DSTV that features Indian movies and series)! Now I was experiencing the real thing.

The hospital seemed like a different planet entirely. I had never seen anything like it in my country. It didn't have the regular hospital smell that I was so used to in Nigeria. We were immediately attended to and, after giving them all my details, I was taken to the ward where I was told that the doctor had been informed of my arrival and would be with me shortly. I was exhausted and lay on the bed (my energy levels had now started to run down so fast). I looked at my dad and he still had a smile on his face. He was a great source of encouragement to me, even in his silence.

Later that night, the oncologist I'd been referred to came to the room to meet with us. He introduced himself saying, 'My name is Dr V. P. Singh and you are Temi.' He had a beautiful smile and a calm aura about him that exuded so much confidence. He had an amazing personality and the weirdest sense of humour for a doctor! He talked us through the process and made it sound like it wasn't difficult at all. I handed all the test results I had brought from Nigeria over to him and he said that while they appreciated this, they would have to run their own tests. These were necessary because if I was ready, they would take me in for surgery the next day. He bade us good night and said that he'd come back in the morning, as he knew we were extremely tired and would need to rest.

The next day he came back to the room and, just like the night before, he cracked some jokes, but then he became serious. He told me about the tests I would have to have done. He also explained the surgical options available and the severity of the disease but assured us that it was nothing to get scared or worried about. He said that he was going to give us till the end of the day to decide which surgical option we were going to pick and, if we were ready and the test results were okay, surgery could happen the next day. It seemed like a whole lot to take in at once, but I knew God wouldn't have brought me this far to leave me. Throughout the whole day, I was taken from one department to the other for different types of tests. The equipment they had in this hospital just blew my mind.

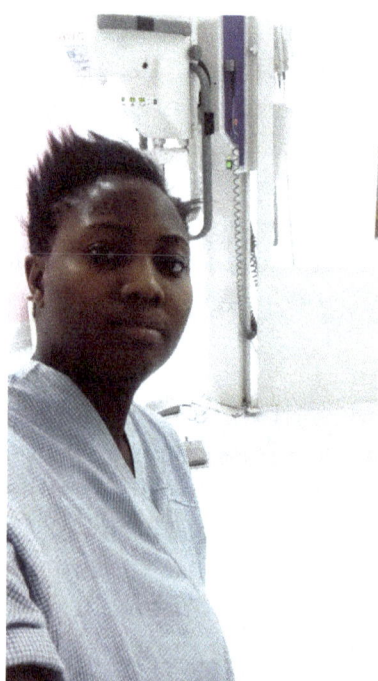
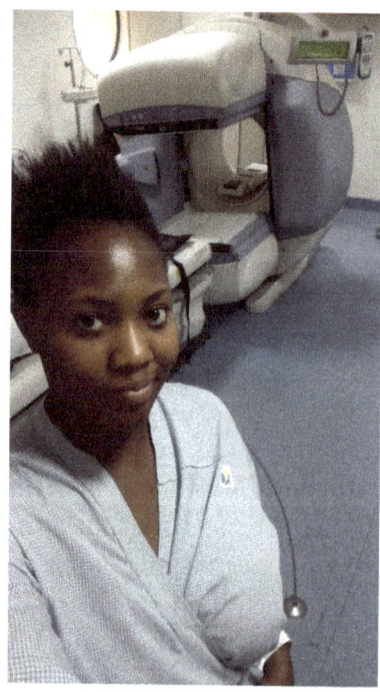

After all the tests I had a lengthy discussion with my dad and we agreed that I was ready, so I was booked for surgery the next day, Saturday 13 February. *Thank God it wasn't Friday the 13th!* I thought. There is a scary myth about Friday the 13th being unlucky and I remembered there was a horror movie about that date too. Funny. Some people have a phobia about Friday the 13th that's called 'Paraskevidekatriaphobia' or 'Friggatriskaidekaphobia'. The type of things some people fear can make one wonder! However, I wasn't afraid, because I knew God had my back.

The method of treatment here was completely different from what I had been used to. Some people may say that it was too soon to be going into the theatre, but what's the point in postponing the 'evil day'? The approach here was quick but I believed the timing was in line with the will of God. A question that a lot of people asked me was, 'Temi, were you scared when you knew you would be taken in for surgery?' My answer was always, 'No, I wasn't scared' simply because I knew God was with me.

Does God feel our pain?

Does God know about what we go through?

Is God aware of our struggles?

These are questions that sometimes go through our minds as humans and the answer to all these questions is a resounding YES. God is aware, He knows, He feels, He cares. He wants to make the load lighter for us to carry. A clear example is found in John 11:35 where we are told that Jesus wept. He knew what was happening to Lazarus. He was aware and He was moved. In several places in the Bible, we read, 'Jesus had compassion'.

All things work according to His perfect will, so no matter what happens remember that God is using you for a greater purpose. The battle is not yours—the battle is the Lord's and He will fight for you. Do not struggle to fight or wage a war, do not try to do

God's work for Him. We are not promised a life without battles but we are assured in God's Word that the battle is not ours but the Lord's.

FEBRUARY 13TH

It was the morning of my surgery. My dad and I had prayed and committed the procedure into the hands of the One who is the greatest physician of all, the One who created me in His image. They came to take me to the theatre. Strangely, I was in very high spirits; I didn't have any fear at all. Yes, that's a true story! I was holding onto the promise God had made to me. He doesn't lie, He doesn't say one thing and do another. He honours His Word more than His Name.

The lady who came to fetch me had such a calm voice. She said, 'You have to take off any undergarments you have on but leave the hospital pyjamas on and turn the shirt to the back.' She asked me which side was affected and I told her the left side so she used a purple marker to mark my left hand. I did as she had said then hugged my daddy. I would have loved to walk into the theatre, but they said it was standard hospital protocol to wheel patients into the theatre. I lay on the stretcher and was wheeled through the long passage. I just saw all the lights on the ceiling go by as I was wheeled past. My dad held my hand and walked with us to the theatre entrance where they told him that he couldn't go any further with us. He said goodbye to me and that he would be waiting for me right outside at this same spot when I came out of the theatre. He had told me he would be fasting alongside me since the doctor had told me that I would have to fast before surgery. At that point, I knew I was committed into God's hands. I was taken to a waiting area where the doctors on my surgery team would come to get acquainted with me and walk me through what to expect. There were several other people lined up for surgeries as well. As I lay there waiting, I could only do one thing— PRAISE.

P — Proclaiming
R — Righteous
A — Acclamation
I — Inspiring
S — Someone's
E — Excellence

I was proclaiming righteous acclamation of God's excellence. The fact that I was in India on its own was a miracle. I don't have to see a jaw-dropping miracle before I praise God or before I worship Him. The mere fact that you are alive is a miracle on its own. I worshipped. I sang Steve Crown's song, *You Are Great*. All I could think of was the greatness of God and the awesomeness of His power.

As I waited, I noticed another man who was waiting to be taken into the theatre. He was so restless. He would stand up and then sit down and lie down and stand up. It was distracting and it was obvious he was scared. When our eyes met, I just smiled at him and that made him smile back at me. At least that calmed him down a little because he became aware that he wasn't the only one there and that made me feel good.

After what seemed like many hours of waiting, I was approached by one of the doctors and the anesthesiologist. They wanted to inform me about the procedure and to find out if I had any drug allergies. Then, at last, I was taken into the theatre with all my test results next to me on the stretcher.

The inside of the theatre was very different from the one I had been taken to in Nigeria. The lights! The lights were so bright. The whole place was completely different from what I had seen back home. I lay there on the operating table and I told God in prayer, 'Lord, unto You I commit myself. Do to me as You will. You are the chief surgeon of this surgery.' The anesthesiologist came to my side and told me he was going to inject what he held in his hand into me and that it was going to make me a bit… Those were the last words I heard.

My throat felt very dry as a result of a tube that had been put into my throat, and which they had just pulled out since I had regained consciousness. I turned my head and I noticed a clock on the wall. 6 pm! Could this time be correct? I thought to myself. My vision was still a bit blurred. I motioned for the nurse to come and I asked her if the time I saw on the clock was correct, and she said that it was. Oh no! My first thought went to my father. I'm sure he must have been worried. But the nurse told me that they had informed my dad about the surgery's success, so with that, I put my mind at rest. I think I must have been in recovery for a couple of hours before I was taken to the ward. The first thing I saw was my father smiling at me.

With gratitude, we said a prayer of thanks to God for a successful surgery.

> *'In everything, give thanks; for this is the will of God in Christ Jesus for you.'* (1 Thessalonians 5:18 NKJV)

RECOVERY PROCESS

The recovery process was an interesting one. I was kept in the ward for just three days and, during that time, I was encouraged to walk around as that was supposed to help me recover.

When you have the right attitude and the right people around you, you heal faster.

My dad had rented a place for us to stay outside the hospital, as the hospital encourages healing outside rather than in the hospital. When we arrived at the guest house, reality struck. It was so different there from how it had been in the hospital. Everything was so difficult! Whilst I'd been in the hospital, I had become used to being treated a certain kind of way with nurses attending to me. Here there were no nurses and no other attendants. It was just my dad and me. This was outside my newfound comfort zone.

COMFORT ZONES

There's something about going out of your comfort zone. Nothing grows in a 'comfort zone'. When you get too comfortable, everything just stagnates. Stepping out of it raises anxiety and generates a stress response, which results in an enhanced level of concentration and focus. It is said that great things are never born in comfort zones. The story of Abraham in the Bible is an instance of this. The first step out of his comfort zone was when he was told to leave his country, his people, and his father's household.

God told Abraham that if he left, He would make him a great nation, bless him and give him a great name. It was something that was going to happen to him, not with Lot, his brother's son who was tagging along with him. God did not reveal the full extent of His promised blessing, nor did He confirm His covenant with Abraham until Lot was gone.

All along the way, God gave Abraham instructions and backed them up with promises. However, what God left out were His reasons. He wanted Abraham to learn to trust His promises even when he didn't know the reason or the details.

When I arrived at the guest house and realised that I wouldn't be able to recline the bed as I had done in the hospital, tears came to my eyes. Then my superhero dad arranged the pillows for me like a ramp so that I could be comfortable. I knew that the healing process had to start; I had to remind myself why my comfort zone had changed and why we'd stepped out of it. Abraham demonstrates that the key to leaving our comfort zone is keeping our eyes on God (Hebrew 11:8-10). When we step outside our comfort zones, we should trust God's promises and anchor our lives in worship. I understand that stepping out is usually not one of the easiest things to do, but we should make sure we keep on moving. This applies to every aspect of our lives—whether it's our business, career or personal growth.

The grass isn't always greener on the other side but we will never know if we never try.

Stepping out of our comfort zones gives God complete leadership of our lives; we give Him charge over us.

> *'Concluding that God was able to raise him up, even from the dead, from which he also received him in a figurative sense.'* (Hebrews 11:19 NKJV)

This was when God had told Abraham to offer up Isaac as a sacrifice. Isaac was Abraham's only begotten son of whom it had been said, *'In Isaac, your seed shall be called'* (Hebrews 11:18 NKJV). Abraham knew that since God was the One Who had given him Isaac as a son, God could still raise him back to life from the dead if he sacrificed him. Learning to trust God is the sole purpose of stepping out of our comfort zones. Let's face it, living by faith means we have to do this. We'd often rather stay comfortable right where we are than grow. It is called a 'comfort zone' for a reason—it is comfortable! If Abraham hadn't left his familiar place and relied fully on God, trusting His guidance, there would have been nothing accounted to him as righteousness as a result of his faith.

Sometimes the Lord may have to move us out of certain situations and places, or away from certain people, to fulfil His promises and His will for our lives. We may be waiting for the blessing to come to us, but there are times we must allow Him to lead us to the blessing. We may not receive it where we are and may be required to go to where it waits. Far too often, we miss an opportunity to be blessed and used of the Lord, simply because we are too afraid to move out of our comfort zones, or too afraid to let go of the things that we are familiar with and venture off to an unknown area. Like baby birds, we are afraid to step out of the nest and truly begin to soar. We want to go, but we want to know the details of the whole master plan first, and almost always want to take a part of the 'comfort zone' with us, something familiar that we can hold onto throughout the journey. However, when the Lord births a great vision in our hearts and declares that He will bring it to pass, He requires us to let go of everything we once held dear and simply BY FAITH follow Him into the unknown.

Just as the Lord was with Abraham, so you can trust Him to be with you and guide you. The God that knows you and loves you wouldn't hang you out to dry. His words and promises are solid. He is faithful and true.

Is the Lord calling you outside of your comfort zone? Will you choose to trust His call and follow Him?

Is He asking you to do something hard?

Listen to Him. He will bring you through and, more often than not, there will be something He'll want to show you along the way. You won't ever be disappointed by taking a leap of faith and getting outside your comfort zone when God is the One who calls you out.

Being diagnosed with cancer wasn't what was taking me to a different place. It was not the thing moving me outside of my comfort zone. Rather, the entire healing process I had to go through is what became my move outside my comfort zone. It meant doing something I had never done before; it meant trusting God in a way I had never done before and it meant depending on Him in a way I'd never had to before. If I wasn't in this situation, I wouldn't know that God could give me the strength to go through this process. That's why I said earlier that you never know how green the grass is on the other side until you go there.

Prayer

Dear Lord,

Thank You that You are a God Who is holy and does not change. I am so glad that You, the all-powerful God of the universe, are also the God who cares about the details of my life. Help me overcome my fear of the unknown and to overcome my reliance on feelings when trying to determine what You desire for me. I trust You to be with me and to guide my step. Teach me to call out to You, to listen for Your answers, and to rely solely on them. I pray in the name of the One who went way out of His comfort zone by dying for my sake, Jesus Christ, Amen.

Little by little, the healing began. Although I had thought it was going to be an extremely difficult process, it turned out not to be so.

Chapter FOUR

ROAD TO RECOVERY

I had two tubes connected to me that were supposed to be draining fluid out of my body. My dad used to joke about this and called them my tail. Daily, we had to drain the fluid that had been collected in the bag.

To be honest, I dreaded nighttime. This sounds strange I know but I didn't like it anytime it was nightfall. The nights seemed so long. Night time was when the devil would try to torment me. Sleep would always be so far away from my eyes but at the first light of day, I would start feeling sleepy. Since I had to stay in a particular position because of the surgery site, lying down as I would have wanted was not possible.

One memorable night in February, when my tubes were still connected to me, it was so difficult getting to sleep. I had tried and tried, but I was in so much pain and sleep wasn't forthcoming. I looked over at my dad and he was sound asleep. How I envied him and wished I was the one doing the sleeping! I asked God to give me sleep because it seemed impossible to fall asleep naturally.

When I woke up in the morning, I said to my dad, 'Thank you for turning me in the night' but to my surprise, he said that he hadn't. Just then, I recalled the experience. Someone had held me and turned me because I'd been feeling very uncomfortable as I lay in the position I was in. The turn was so obvious and had put me into a very comfortable position so that I could sleep. It could only have been God.

God uses the most mundane things to speak to us and to let us know that He is with us. He is completely aware of whatever it is we are going through, and He understands our feelings.

Many days passed and I was gradually getting better. Day by day, I noticed improvements. It was time for chemotherapy to be administered to me again. When we arrived at the hospital, we were given a room. The tubes were taken out because my wounds had started to heal well and no more fluid was draining out. You will recall that I'd had my first round of chemo in Nigeria, as my professor had advised. I was supposed to have a total of eight cycles, so technically I still had seven left. My medical oncologist had asked me to give him the prescription of the first chemotherapy I'd had in Nigeria. I didn't have it with me but I remembered I had taken a photo of the prescription the day it had been administered to me. I checked through my phone and showed the picture to him. He looked at it and asked, 'Is this what you were given?' I told him it was. He looked at me in surprise and said, 'You are lucky your heart is in very good working condition because this combination was wrong and could have given you a cardiac arrest.' I was shocked and scared at the same time but I was grateful to God that my heart was strong.

My dad looked at me in relief and was also thankful to God that nothing had gone wrong. No wonder my complexion had turned darker just two days after the chemo had been administered to me in Nigeria! The second chemo session went well and I was discharged from the hospital the same day.

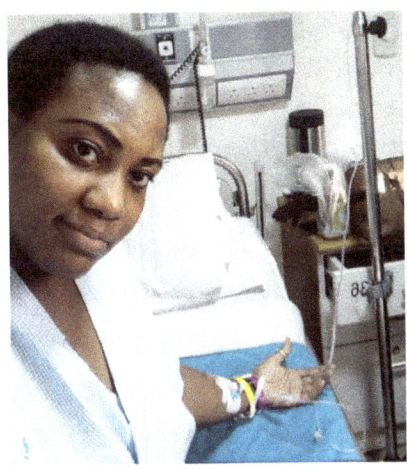
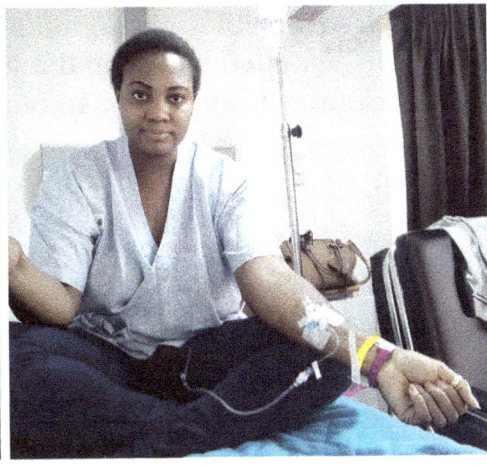

Soon afterwards, as so often happens, I reacted to the chemotherapy. Now, chemotherapy causes a lot of different reactions for different people. The next day was when reality struck. I felt nauseous and vomited. I felt tired and weak; strength and virtue were leaving me, so to speak. I was reminded of the story of Paul in the Bible. Paul was considered by the Corinthians to be a weak person, lacking the charisma which they possessed. He didn't have poise and lacked confidence. Radically, Paul embraced all the things that the Corinthians rejected about him, identifying these as signs of his true apostleship. He argued that his weakness was verification that the power of God working through him, and he rejected the Corinthians' view of power as worldly success, bravery and status. Even in his weakness, Paul could speak of his strength.

> *'And lest I should be exalted above measure by the abundance of the revelations, a thorn in the flesh was given to me, a messenger of Satan to buffet me, lest I be exalted above measure. Concerning this thing, I pleaded with the Lord three times that it might depart from me. And He said to me, My grace is sufficient for you, for My strength is made perfect in weakness. Therefore, most gladly I will rather boast in my infirmities, that the power of Christ may rest upon me. Therefore, I take pleasures in infirmities, in reproaches, in needs, in persecutions and distress, for Christ's sake. For when I am weak, then I am strong.' (2 Corinthians 12:7-10 NKJV)*

Paul viewed weakness as an embracing of strength because in weakness he depended upon the strength of God. His weakness was the source of his power. In our times of trouble, embracing weakness and depending on God's power is the way of life that all Christians are called to live. As Christians, we are called to embrace and acknowledge our weakness even as Jesus did.

> *'For though He was crucified in weakness, yet He lives by the power of God...' (2 Corinthians 13:4 NKJV)*

This reliance on the power of God in times when we are weak is our calling in Christ today as well. For we gain our lives only when we lose them for Christ's sake (Matthew 16:25). We are called not to rely on ourselves, but upon God who raises the dead (2 Corinthians 1:9). We do not look to ourselves for the strength to overcome sin, become a better person, get healed or establish a successful organisation. We do not appeal to our strengths and abilities to get things done. This is a call to look to God alone because besides Him we can do nothing—but in Him, we bear fruits (John 15:5). When we embrace our weakness and trust in the power of God, we bear witness to Christ in a world obsessed with all forms of power that exist. When we embrace our weakness and abide in God's strength, we bring glory to Him.

The next couple of days passed by slowly; my strength was gradually coming back to me. The doctors had advised that I take in a lot of fluids, but honestly, drinking water wasn't a priority on my list. Even the thought of food put me off it completely. However, I had to force myself to drink the fluids, as it wouldn't make sense to treat the cancer and then create problems for other organs in my body like my kidneys and liver. One of the days, my dad and I went to the hospital to meet with the doctors for a routine check-up. After that had been done, we were leaving the hospital when we were stopped by a polite lady who greeted us and asked us which country we were from. We said that we were Nigerians and she said that she was from Nigeria as well. 'I was diagnosed with Stage-3 breast cancer and I have come here for treatment,' she told us. She quickly took off the wig she was wearing and we saw that her head was completely shaved. She told us that her name was Chika and spoke of her diagnosis, probably so I would be comfortable talking about mine. I told her that I had also been diagnosed with Stage-3 breast cancer and had already had my surgery. Chika asked that we meet her husband and we went to meet with him. We introduced ourselves and told them where we were staying. They said that they'd come and visit us later after their doctor's appointment.

They came around later that day and we got talking. She shared her experiences so far and told us she'd had two cycles of chemotherapy in Nigeria. She'd had to leave her five-month-old baby back in Nigeria to come for treatment. From that day, we became friends with their family. They were the first Nigerian couple we met in India and it was really lovely to have met with them. They were also extremely excited about meeting with us and moved into the same hotel we were staying in. My dad and the lady's husband were really happy as both of them had had concerns about how we would be able to cope whilst on treatment in a foreign land all alone. We then decided that when my dad and her husband went back to Nigeria, Chika and I would move in together and stay as roommates. We even talked about splitting the room rent, which was more convenient for all of us. The lady kept asking me how I felt and what I was experiencing. It was some sort of fear she had, which is only normal. After all, we are all human. I reassured her that it was something that she would go through without stress.

She had her surgery and it was successful, all thanks to God. My dad had to go back to Nigeria and so did her husband, so we moved in together. Ultimately, we became each other's support. Because she was older than me and as a mark of respect, I referred to her as 'Aunty Chika'. When I was down from chemo, she would support me and when she was down from her chemo, I would support her. It would have been very lonely if we hadn't paired up. We encouraged each other and prayed together; we built each other up and ate together. God knows how to be there for the people who love Him.

> *'And we know that all things work together for good to those who love God, to those who are called according to His purpose.' (Romans 8:28 NKJV)*

God never leaves us stranded or in a situation where there won't be a way of escape. There's a practical example of this in the Bible—the story of Joseph in Genesis 37. Joseph was the eleventh son of Jacob and the first born of his mother Rachel. His father was about ninety years old when he was born. Joseph was Rachel's favourite son and she was his father's favourite wife. He had one brother and ten half-brothers, but that's not all there is to know about Joseph. He was a dreamer and an interpreter of dreams. This was his talent; his God-given gift which he put to good use despite his brothers' annoyance. Joseph's father Jacob made a coat of many colours for him. His brothers were jealous and because of the hatred his brothers had for him, they plotted amongst themselves that they would kill him, throw him into a pit and tell their father he'd been attacked by wild beasts.

Joseph went out to find his brothers in the fields because their father sent him there with food for them. The brothers eventually didn't kill him, but they sold him off as a slave. They took his colourful coat, soaked it in the blood of a goat's kid and told their father he'd been killed by wild beasts.

Poor Joseph's story didn't end there. Although he was now a slave, God blessed him and favoured him. The Egyptian who'd bought Joseph, Potiphar, had noticed Joseph was blessed and highly favoured, and picked him out of the many slaves to be in charge of the household. Joseph's master's wife lusted after him because he was very handsome in form and appearance. *'Lie with me'*, she said to him but Joseph refused and said to her, *'My master does not know what is with me in the house, and he has committed all that he has to my hand. There is no one greater than I, nor has he kept back anything from me but you, because you are his wife. How then can I do this great wickedness, and sin against God?' (Genesis 39:7-9 NKJV)*. The woman kept on speaking with him as the days went by. She tried her luck again, but this time Joseph fled and left his cloak behind because she was holding onto it. She later told her husband that he had tried to have his way with her, but that she had screamed and he'd fled, forgetting to take his cloak with him. On hearing this, Potiphar became angry and demanded that Joseph be thrown into prison. Even that wasn't the end of his misery, but what could have been a disaster turned out to be a blessing in disguise for him, as that was where his elevation came from when he was later put in charge of the whole of Egypt, under Pharoah.

It is often difficult for us to look beyond our current situation or circumstances. We forget that while it seems as though we are doing nothing useful, God is working for our good, if only we put our faith and trust in Him. Many blessings in life don't look like blessings at first. For some reason, we have the idea that when we ask God to be a part of our lives, He is going to make things pleasant all the time. We pray for blessings all the time in our lives, but how do we react when God does things to produce in us the things that will bless us in the future? What happens when we receive blessings in disguise? Do we even recognise them? God desires to bless us all the time but sometimes, to receive His blessings, we need to have a crisis first. It is often said that before there can be a testimony, there will be a test. That's why sometimes our misery turns into our blessing. Look beyond the way things are and learn to trust and have faith in God.

The plans God has for us don't just include 'good things', but the whole array of human events. God talks about prosperity in the book of Jeremiah; just that the prospering that is talked about is often the outcome of a 'bad event'. Sometimes, instead of just demanding more and more from God and asking Him to fix whatever difficult circumstance we may find ourselves in, we should rather thank Him and be thankful for His presence as we go through the situation. We know that He has said, *'I will never leave you nor forsake you'* (Hebrews 13:5b NKJV). Since we have the assurance of His presence with us, we should face every situation in life knowing that God is with us. We can learn of God's presence in our lives through trials and struggles, and that's when we develop our spiritual muscles. If we go to the gym for the first time and workout for one hour straight, the next day and even the day after, we will feel pain in places we never knew existed. The pains come as a result of the workout we did, working on muscles that we haven't worked before. The pains will come—they're a natural phenomenon after such rigorous training—but don't give up and don't get discouraged. It's better to get the muscles in good shape, even though it will cost us pain and effort. The same also applies to our spiritual development. In tough times, we are forced to rely solely on God. When our blessings are disguised as trials and struggles, God wants to bless our lives with endurance and confidence in Him. He wants us to fully trust and rely on Him.

COMPLETE RELIANCE ON GOD

You rely on things you believe in and fully trust. Many people place their trust in the wrong things. Many have entrusted the salvation of their souls to man, rather than placing their trust in God.

God asks the question, 'Do you trust Me?' He wants you to trust Him completely.

Many believe in God, they believe He exists, but they do not rely on Him. I am encouraging you to rely solely on God. Put your trust in Him because His way is perfect even when we feel as though things are not going the way they should, or it looks as though the world is crumbling down on us.

The Lord is good; He is a stronghold in the day of trouble but I tell you, He can only deliver you in the day of trouble if you rely on Him. Do not rely on man. Listen to what the psalmist wrote in Psalm 118:8-9:

> *'It is better to trust in the Lord than to put confidence in man.*
> *It is better to trust in the Lord than to put confidence in princes.'*
> *(NKJV)*

False religion is some form of relying on man's doctrine rather than God's. True religion comes from God and false religion is from man. Some groups of people follow some written or unwritten rules produced by man, rather than the Word of God. Christians believe in the Bible—the Word of God.

To trust in man is to depart from God. The Word of God speaks of the man who makes flesh his strength and whose heart departs from the Lord as one who is cursed, and such a man shall not see good when it comes (Jeremiah 17:5-6).

Several methods can be used as a source of our reliance on God because sometimes doing the same thing over and over can make things too monotonous and boring. If you are wondering what tools you can use to help you rely on God completely, there are two things you could explore.

1) PRAYER as a source of reliance on God

> *'Trust in the Lord with all your heart*
> *and lean not on your own understanding;*
> *in all your ways acknowledge Him,*
> *and He shall direct your paths.'*
> *(Proverbs 3:5-6 NKJV)*

Prayer, by its very nature, moves us away from our reliance on ourselves and towards reliance on God. This text from the book of Proverbs instructs us in this basic wisdom. 'Trust in the Lord,' it says. Rely on God, lean on God; turn to God for wisdom, guidance and help.

The text goes on to tell us that as we lean on God, we are to lean away from our understanding. This does not mean that being people of faith requires us to leave our brains at the door. It means that we remember that God is God, and we are not. It means that we live with the reality of our limits. It means that we keep in mind how limited our understanding is, how limited our knowledge is, how limited we are in our ability to manage our lives on our own.

The image of leaning on God and the image of leaning on our own understanding represent two different paths for life. The path we are most familiar with is the path of trying to figure everything out and trying to get it all right. The most used path is the path of relying on our own strength and understanding. The path of leaning on God — of trusting God with all our heart — is the path less travelled by most of us.

The wisdom of giving up self-reliance and learning to rely on God in all we do is counter-intuitive for most of us. We have been taught to value self-reliance, to see it as the goal of human development. We have not been taught to value reliance on others, not even reliance on God.

Even within our church circles, we have lost the core value and practice of reliance on God rather than reliance on ourselves. Prayer, Scripture reading and other religious practices have become activities we do as a kind of performance to win God's approval. It's almost as though we are just marking the register or performing a tick-box exercise. The things that are meant to open our hearts to the love and wisdom of God become things we do to feel that we are doing all the right things and jumping through all the right hoops.

Prayer is not a performance to pacify an angry or demanding God. Prayer in all its essence is an acknowledgement of our need for God. Prayer is child-like trust in a loving God who desires to guide and bless us.

All of Scripture tells us that life was meant to be lived in full, joyful reliance on the One who made us and Who is with us always. Life was meant to be lived in vital, intimate, daily turning to God in all we do, knowing our need for God and trusting that He will make a clear path before us.

According to the wisdom of this text from the book of Proverbs, relying on God is a matter of the heart. We trust God with our whole heart. Relying on God rather than on ourselves means we give our heart to God; we give our love to God. We do this because God has already given His heart to us. It was the ultimate sacrifice on the cross for us and because God loves us dearly, we can entrust Him with our hearts and lives.

I do not have to know it all, understand it all, figure it all out or even look for a solution to anything, as long as my reliance is on God.

Prayer

Dear Lord,

I often strive to control things that are not within my control. I try to figure out matters that are beyond understanding. But I can let go of my attempts to be in charge. I can let go of reliance on myself and begin to rely on you instead. You know, You see, You understand and You invite me to lean on You, to let You guide me. Please teach me to give up my reliance on myself and my reliance on man, because reliance on man takes the glory away from You. Dear Lord, teach me to trust You with my whole heart and to seek Your guidance in all I do.

Amen.

Prayer suggestion: In your free time, here are some prayer suggestions that could help you to pray aright.

- Talk to God about the fears that make it difficult for you to trust Him with all your heart.
- Talk to God about your desire to trust Him with all your heart and all your soul.
- Ask God to help you give up your reliance on self and man.
- Ask God to increase your capacity to trust Him and His timing.
- Ask God for help and guidance in all you do today.

2) PRAISE as a source of reliance on God

Praise is one of the main reasons we were created. We can see several instances in the Bible where it speaks about the place of praise and worship.

> *'And do not be drunk with wine, in which is dissipation, but be filled with the Spirit, speaking to one another in psalms and hymns and spiritual songs, singing and making melody in your heart to the Lord.' (Ephesians 5:18-19 NKJV)*

Praise and worship trigger the overflow of God's Spirit in our hearts. We not only enter God's presence through praise (Psalm 100:4), but we are also filled with His presence through worship. Are you feeling empty within? Worship God with all your heart and the Spirit of the living God will fill your innermost being.

> *'Draw near to God and He will draw near to you.' (James 4:8 NKJV)*

> *'If anyone is thirsty, let him come to Me and drink. He who believes in Me, as the Scripture said, "From his innermost being will flow rivers of living water." But this He spoke of the Spirit, whom those who believed in Him were to receive…' (John 7:37-39 NASB)*

Praise is also the response to being filled with God's Spirit, Who cries out from within us in prayer and praise.

> *'Ye have received the Spirit of adoption, whereby we cry, Abba, Father!' (Romans 8:15b KJV)*

> *'And because you are sons, God has sent forth the Spirit of His Son into your hearts, crying, "Abba, Father!"' (Galatians 4:6 NKJV)*

Throughout Scripture, we read of people worshipping and magnifying God when they were filled with the Holy Spirit. Worship is an evidence of a Spirit-filled life. As the Holy Spirit flows within our hearts, the natural response of the human spirit is praise and worship.

> *'And those of the circumcision who believed were astonished, as many as came with Peter, because the gift of the Holy Spirit had been poured out on the Gentiles also.' (Acts 10:45 NKJV)*

Praise draws you close to God. It helps you to fix your focus on God, thereby making you rely on Him. It helps you feel and experience Him, which in turn automatically creates an atmosphere for hearing from God.

If you want to hear from God, you must praise and worship Him. Acts 13:2 says, *'While they were ministering to the Lord and fasting, the Holy Spirit said...' (NASB)*

When I am in a service where the praise and worship are intense, I feel the greatest anointing. It is in this type of atmosphere that God seems to speak the clearest. Whether in your time with God, or a public setting, praise is the key to hearing from Him.

We also find this when we are in a spiritual battle. It is when we are going through a time of difficulty and spiritual conflict that we desperately need to hear from God. In 2 Kings 3:9, Ahab and Jehoshaphat ran out of water while going to battle against Moab. Jehoshaphat said, *'Is there not a prophet of the Lord here that we may inquire by him?'* One of the king's servants said, *'Elisha the son of Shaphat is here.'* Jehoshaphat said, *'The Word of the Lord is with him.' (2 Kings 3:11-12 NKJV)*

They went to Elisha and he told them, *'Bring me a minstrel.'* After the minstrel played Elisha proclaimed, *'Thus says the Lord.'* It was only after the musician began to play that the Lord spoke to Elisha, who gave them the Word of God they needed for victory. This is why it is important to praise. Praise and worship usher in the anointing and presence of God, not only in a church service but also in our personal quiet time. We should always have a time of praise and worship before we study the Word, whether it is in a corporate setting or our devotions.

Praise as a remedy for anxiety

> 'Do not be anxious about anything, but in every situation, by prayer and petition, with thanksgiving, present your requests to God. And the peace of God, which transcends all understanding, will guard your hearts and your minds in Christ Jesus.' (Philippians 4:6-7 NIV)

The prescription for anxiety in Philippians 4:6-8 is prayer, praise and a positive mindset. We need to be *'casting all our care upon Him, for He cares for us'* (1 Peter 5:7). That said, prayer alone is not enough. Prayer focuses on the problem, whereas praise focuses on the solution. Prayer keeps our concentration on the cause of our anxiety. It is important to pray, but don't stop there. We must always move from prayer to praise, so we do not dwell on the problem but the solution. In Matthew 11:28-29, Jesus said, *'Come to Me, all you who labor and are heavy laden, and I will give you rest. Take My yoke upon you and learn from Me, for I am gentle and lowly in heart, and you will find rest for your souls.'* (NKJV)

Praise activates blessings

Think about how you feel when someone tells you how great you are. Our immediate response might be, 'What do you want?' We laugh, but if they are constantly praising us, we usually give them anything they want.

God is the same. If we are continually praising and worshipping Him, telling Him how much we love Him and how great He is, He is likely to give us anything we desire (Psalm 37:4), sometimes even before we ask.

> *'It shall also come to pass that before they call, I will answer; and while they are still speaking, I will hear.'* (Isaiah 65:24 AMP)

How wonderful is that? Praise brings this to fulfilment in our lives. If we would spend more time in praise and worship, we would have a lot less to pray about.

Praise gives us victory over our enemies

In 2 Chronicles 20:12, the enemy was coming against the people of God and Jehoshaphat was afraid and prayed, *'We have no power against this great multitude that is coming against us; nor do we know what to do, but our eyes are upon You.'* (NKJV)

As humans, we have all been in a place where we were afraid, felt completely overwhelmed, or had no idea what to do. That is exactly the position God's people were in here. It was only when they praised the Lord with all of their hearts that He struck down the enemy. They did not even have to lift a hand to fight.

Also, their praise was not timid and ritualistic. They *'stood up to praise the Lord God of Israel with a very loud voice'* (2 Chronicles 20:19 AMP). They praised Him with all their might, and as a result, God fought for them, struck down their enemy, and gave them victory.

In Exodus 17:10-13, we read about when Amalek fought against Israel at Rephidim. Moses sent Joshua to fight for Israel while he stood on top of the hill with Aaron and Hur. When Moses held up his hands, Israel prevailed. When he lowered his hands, Amalek prevailed. When Moses grew weary, Aaron and Hur held up his hands, allowing Joshua to overwhelm Amalek. In Exodus 17:15, it is written that Moses built an altar and named it Jehovah-Nissi, 'The Lord is my banner.' As long as Moses kept his hands lifted high in praise, Israel prevailed against the enemy. The same is true for us. If we constantly praise and worship Him, God will cause us to prevail and our enemies will flee before us. As we fully rely on Him, we should remember to lift His banner high and unashamedly for all to see.

In the book of Acts, we read about how when it was about midnight, Paul and Silas were praying and singing hymns to God while they were in jail. The other prisoners were listening to them (Acts 16:25). We may wonder how Paul and Silas could sing at such a difficult time. Didn't they know they were unfairly chained up in a prison? Paul and Silas could praise God because they were filled with faith and with the Holy Spirit.

Faith *is being sure of what we hope for. It is being certain of what we do not see.* (Hebrews 11:1). Paul and Silas were SURE that God had not forgotten them. They were CERTAIN that God would not allow anything that was not His BEST for them to happen. And they were filled with the **Holy Spirit.** One of the fruits of the Holy Spirit is **joy** (Galatians 5:22). Please notice that I did not say 'happiness'. Joy is different from happiness. Happiness comes when your circumstances are good—such as when you get a gift, or you get a contract. Joy comes when things are right on the inside—it is the inner gladness and peace you have because you believe in Jesus. Joy doesn't change when our circumstances change. Joy is found deep down inside of us. Out of joy, given by the Holy Spirit, Paul and Silas praised the Lord .

The book of Acts goes on to tell us that suddenly there was a powerful earthquake that shook the prison from top to bottom. All at once, the prison doors flew open. Everybody's chains came loose (Acts 16:26). It is important to note that it was while the two men were singing praises that the ground started to move. God shook the earth on behalf of those He wanted to save! Rock walls tumbled and metal scraped against metal. Chains fell to the ground, and heavy doors swung open. Paul and Silas could have easily run into the darkness of the night and escaped. However, the two men were listening to the Holy Spirit; they did not run away after the chains fell off and the doors opened. The Holy Spirit let them know that God had not caused this amazing earthquake just to set them free—God had sent the earthquake to set the jailer free!

How do you react to hard times or unfair treatment? Do those around you hear you complain like everybody else? Or do they hear you pray and praise God? Even though Paul and Silas were treated most unfairly, because of the joy of the Holy Spirit inside them, they praised God instead of grumbling. Paul and Silas were not singing in church, they were singing in the darkest place. As a result, the other people in that dark place heard their praise; they heard the truth about the mighty, living God. Later, Paul wrote:

> *'Do all things without complaining and disputing, that you may become blameless and harmless, children of God without fault in the midst of a crooked and perverse generation, among whom you shine as lights in the world, holding fast the word of life.' (Philippians 2:14-16a NKJV)*

Anyone can complain. Only those who are filled with the Holy Spirit can give God thanks and praise when times are difficult. When you do this in the darkest places, you will shine like a bright star in the darkest night. Others will see you and be drawn to the One you praise. Don't forget, your praise invites God's earth-quaking power into every situation!

Praise does so much. Total reliance on God means we give our time, our praise, our prayer, amongst other things to Him. And when we do, He will give us a ground-breaking miracle.

Chapter FIVE

SUPPORT SYSTEMS

I was at the International Patients Lounge (IPL) one day when I overheard some people talking about the situation in Nigeria. I was so excited to find other Nigerians in a foreign country and they were also happy to have the chance at a discussion in the northern language (Hausa). Coincidentally, I also understand the language, so I decided to identify with them. We all exchanged pleasantries and somehow, we all got talking. Some days after that, I bumped into one of the people we had met at the IPL and it felt good to see him. Everyone called him 'Uncle Adamu'. He happened to live in the same town where I had been born and raised and where my parents live—the city of Jos. We had such an amazing time talking about the beauty, peace and clean air that is found in Jos. His mother was on treatment for cancer at the hospital as well, so I went with him to say hello to her. Such amazing people. Sometimes he would come to visit me in the hospital during my chemo days, and he also came to visit my roommate and me in our room. It helped things to not feel so bad and made the place more like a home away from home.

As time went on, the treatment didn't feel as long as it had seemed when I had just started. I felt stronger day by day. I made more friends who were all either patients themselves or attendants and all wonderful people. I met and became friends with Emmy, Nayon, Rashida, Uncle Chinedu and his wife, Mr Gabriel and his wife, to mention a few. They all had unique sides to them. Nayon still struck me as the most amazing out of them all. She had such a big, motherly heart. She called me 'my girly girly'—I was just like a daughter to her. She would call me to make sure I had eaten and taken my drugs and would always want to make sure I was alright. On several of my chemo days, she would tell my roommate to go and rest and that she would stay with me in the hospital. I also reciprocated her gesture;

we all looked out for one another's welfare. We used to go to church together and made some good friends there too. Well, that was after we had a funny episode in church...

One Sunday, I had worn a wig to go to church and had used a small scarf to tie over it. I did that rather than cover it up completely because most times I couldn't bear the heat that was emanating from my bald head because of the clinical menopause I was having due to the chemotherapy. I used to become extremely hot and to make matters worse, it was the middle of summer in Delhi. On this particular day, when Nayon and I arrived at church, the ushers came to tell me that I need to cover my head fully. I tried to explain to them why I wasn't going to be able to cover it all up but they obviously didn't know that I was a patient. I became so upset that I took off the wig since I couldn't have the wig on and have my head completely covered up as well. Everyone saw my bald head which made me so emotional that I started to cry. Nayon felt my pain and she too, in a bid to console me, started to cry. Eventually, we managed to stop crying. Brother Eugene had noticed what was going on and came to speak to us, apologising that he hadn't known that we were going through anything at all. Well, that was how we made friends in church. The friends from church were so nice; they called often and came around to visit us and pray with us.

The devil doesn't stop when he sees that we are winning. In fact, it is at such times that he starts to try even harder. My treatment was going well until I started to react to the chemo drug that I was being given. It was strange because I had received this drug before and nothing like this had happened. My whole body started to itch so badly that I resorted to using something with a sharp edge—like a knife—to scratch myself. Then my whole body started to change colour. It was a horrible feeling. On three occasions, I had to be rushed to the emergency unit at the hospital where I was given an antipruritic medicine intravenously, which reduced the effect of the itching. This reaction started from the sixth chemo cycle and continued until after the seventh. I'd had enough of it by then; it didn't matter where I was or who I was with when the itching started, it was like all hell had broken loose and I resembled a mad person with the way I scratched myself. I had just one chemo cycle left when I decided that I wasn't going to go through the same thing again. Everyone around me wondered what I was going to do, but I kept my intended action to myself.

I patiently waited till it was time for my eighth and final chemo cycle and went to the hospital to be admitted before the administration of chemo was due to start. My medical oncologist, Dr P. K Das came around to do his consultation before they administered the chemo and, since he was aware of the reaction I had been having, he offered me a solution. He said, 'Since this drug is causing this reaction, we can change it; it's still the same drug but just a different brand.' I considered it for a minute and then he mentioned that the only problem was that the new drug was much more expensive than the one used previously. After hearing that, I told the doctor not to worry and that I would use the old one. He then asked, 'But what about the reaction you have been having?' I told him not to worry about that because this time around I wouldn't be getting any reaction. He looked at me, smiled and said that he trusted me. He didn't quite understand why I'd said that or what I was going to do differently. That day, Nayon was the one who stayed with me in the hospital for my chemo.

When it was time for them to connect the drip to the cannula that had already been inserted into my vein, I told the nurse to give me a few minutes. I told her that I would call her back when I was ready so she left us alone. Nayon was wondering why I needed a few minutes and asked me what was happening. I told her that I had decided that this time around the chemo wasn't going to itch as it had done with the past two administrations and she asked, 'So what will you do?' I reached for my bag and brought out my anointing oil. It had a sweet-smelling fragrance of frankincense and myrrh and had been a gift from my father which he'd brought back from his pilgrimage to Israel. I told Nayon that the Bible helps me to understand

> *'that at the name of Jesus every knee should bow, of those in heaven, and of those on earth, and of those under the earth, and that every tongue should confess that Jesus Christ is Lord, to the glory of God the Father.' (Philippians 2:10-11 NKJV)*

I took the anointing oil, anointed the chemo bottle and prayed, 'I anoint this chemo in the name of the Father, the Son and the Holy Spirit. Hear the word of the Lord: you shall not cause me any allergy, you shall do only what you are supposed to do in my body, and not cause me harm or hurt. I take authority over you and command you to be safe in my body, in the name of Jesus.' We said Amen and then called the nurse to come and connect the chemo to my cannula. It all looked like a trick when I was discharged from the hospital and went back home. I shared the experience with my roommate but she had some doubts. 'Let's wait and see,' she said sceptically.

'Yes, we shall see,' I replied. The first day after chemo passed and then the second day, and the third day. No itching. Whenever I was with my roommate and needed to clean sweat from my face or do something that would require me to raise my hand, she would ask, 'Has the itching started?' I would answer, 'No, it is not itching and it will not start.' That is the power of being positive, for as we say it, it happens to us. When they say there's a casting down, we should say there is a lifting up of heads. Even one of my doctors who saw me often would demonstrate with her hands, mimicking how I used to vigorously scratch my whole body. She would ask me, 'Has it started?' and I would reply, 'It won't start.' I remember one time she said, 'Well, if it hasn't started yet, let's give it some time and see what happens on the seventh to the tenth days. I still told her that it wouldn't happen this time around. Everyone around me was counting the days along with me. The twelfth day came and went and there was no itching at all. It was a miracle that God had performed. We should recognise the power that we possess as children of God; the power of good and evil is in the tongue and we should learn to speak positively, even in the face of the toughest situation.

Chemotherapy was finally over; I was the happiest person in the whole hospital that day! I didn't know if I should shout or if I should cry. A huge hurdle had been crossed at last.

The treatment wasn't over yet, but I was closer to the end than from when I'd started. My next appointment with the doctors was two weeks later and I was doing well. I was then referred to the radiation oncologist. Radiation, or radiotherapy, was the last phase of my treatment. Radiation is a type of treatment that uses high-energy waves to shrink tumours and kill cancer cells. I was informed about what the process entailed including the side effects and reactions. They had to build a protective cast over my body to protect other parts from being affected by the radiation.

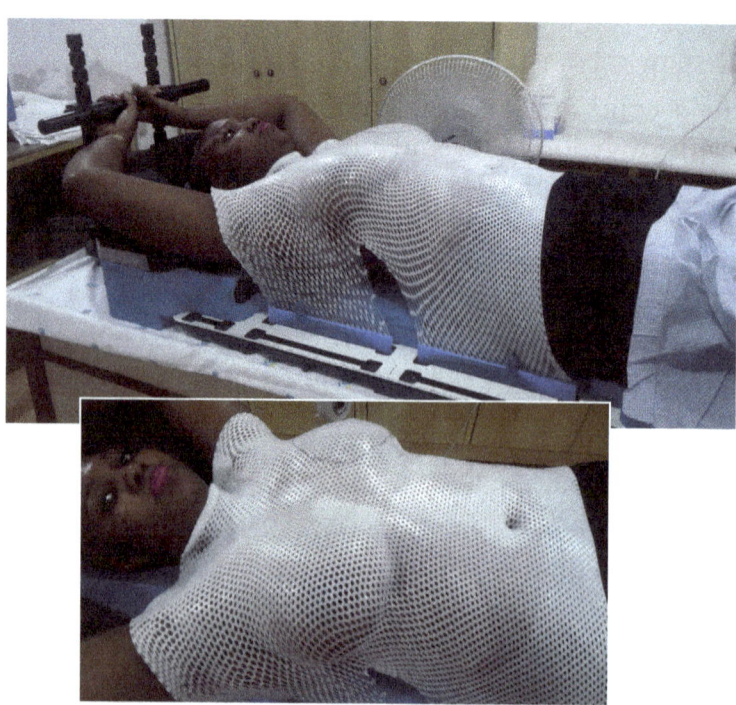

The radiation treatment started and I found out, just as they'd informed me, that it was absolutely painless. However, it comes with its own troubles as it causes nausea, weakness, extreme tiredness, and can give burns. It has long-term side effects that don't go away so quickly. I had twenty radiation sessions. It wasn't the easiest thing to go through, but God was with me through the process.

September 1, 2016

BabyTinks' post on Breastcancer.org discussion forum:

It's been a month since I finished my treatment. Lumpectomy with LD Flap reconstruction, chemotherapy and radiation, and I'm not able to get over all I had to go through. Sometimes, I just get lost in my thoughts. My skin hasn't changed after radiation and I have pains and swelling in my left breast by the side closest to my armpit. I have gotten my periods back, but they are still very unusual—very heavy bleeding. My hair is growing again, yaaaaay! I want to be around people but I also don't want any sort of sympathy from them; it's cancer not a death sentence I mean. Am I the only one who feels this way? And I keep asking myself, 'What next? Now what?'

DEALING WITH UNEXPECTED NEWS

We may pause to wonder why sometimes certain things just don't go away right after a prayer or during prayers. We would agree that sometimes we expect one thing but get something else at the end. It could be a doctor's report, a pregnancy test result, a job interview, money—you name it. Sometimes we get what we expect and other times, we get what we do not expect. It can be very disappointing when we get what we do not expect. The doctors can tell you, 'Sorry, you can never get pregnant.' Don't beat yourself up. It's just the doctor's report. God didn't say it to you, so why worry?

I remember the time when the doctors told me, 'Ma'am, you've got cancer, and it's in the third stage.' I felt as though the world had come to an end. It wasn't what I was expecting to hear, but I had to brace myself and fight cancer like a warrior. Now my treatment was over and I thought that was it. I was in for a shock. I went back for my checkup and the doctor said to me, 'I'm sorry, but the disease has spread to your liver and your bone.' This was certainly not what I'd expected to hear, but I decided that I'd do what I had to do. I'd have to fight again.

Don't let anything or any unexpected news deal negatively with you. Do not let it disturb your peace of mind. Storms come our way to test our sails. The winds must blow, the waves must come. Franklin D Roosevelt once said, 'A smooth sea never made a skilled sailor.'

There's always a counter-reaction for everything.

Try praise.

Try thanksgiving.

Try to make yourself as happy as you can be.

Until the expected news you are waiting for comes, don't stop trying. It is said, 'While you are waiting for God to open a door for you, praise Him in the hallway.'

Never stop trusting. Never stop believing. Trust God.

Temi's writing journey ends here.

EVEN IF...

Let's take a step back to the book of Daniel and focus on three friends—Shadrach, Meshach and Abednego. King Nebuchadnezzar had appointed these three young Jewish men as chief ministers over the province of Babylon at the request of Daniel their friend, after he'd not only told the king what he (the king) had dreamt but had also given the meaning of the dream to him, thus saving all the wise men of Babylon from execution. Now, these same young Jewish men had the guts to disobey a direct order of the king. What a way to treat someone who has promoted you! So, why did they do it? What or who gave them the boldness?

The king had made an image of gold and set it up in Babylon. He'd then commanded that all the leaders and provincial officials of the land, as well as the people, be present for the dedication of the image. To further degrade them and make sure they knew who was boss, he had the herald make a proclamation commanding them to fall and worship the image of gold at the sound of the musical instruments. But he had forgotten one tiny detail, or perhaps he was not aware that many years before, God had spoken to the Israelites when He'd given them the ten commandments saying:

> *'I am the LORD your God, who brought you out of Egypt, out of the land of slavery. You shall have no other gods before me. You shall not make for yourselves an image in the form of anything in heaven above or on the earth beneath or in the waters below. You shall not bow down to them or worship them; for I, the LORD your God, am a jealous God, punishing the children for the sin of the parents to*

> *the third and fourth generation of those who hate me, but showing love to a thousand generations of those who love me and keep my commandments.' (Exodus 20:2-6 NIV)*

Shadrach, Meshach and Abednego did not forget. They did not sell their birthright and that is what gave them the boldness to disobey the king. They knew that the God they served was more powerful than a mere man who had deluded himself and all his followers into thinking that he was something he was not. This, despite the fact that he'd only recently proclaimed God as 'The God of gods and the Lord of kings and the revealer of mysteries' (Daniel 2:47 NIV). They knew what was at stake. They knew that they could lose their lives and become ash in a matter of minutes. They knew that the king was a no-nonsense man. But these men also knew the God whom they served. These young men could stand assured in the knowledge of the God they had trusted in and proclaim without fear.

> *'King Nebuchadnezzar, we do not need to defend ourselves before you in this matter. If we are thrown into the blazing furnace, the God we serve is able to deliver us from it and He will deliver us from your Majesty's hand. But even if he does not, we want you to know, Your Majesty, that we will not serve your gods or worship the image of gold you have set up.' (Daniel 3:16-18 NIV)*

Shadrach, Meshach and Abednego were confident that God could deliver them from the burning furnace. They were also confident that even if He did not deliver them, they would not disappoint Him by bowing down to another god. This was my stance too. I remember several 'advisers' coming with different suggestions on how I could get healed of cancer. Some involved going to see some strange prophets or performing some sacrifice. I had to tell them to their faces that I trusted God to heal me and if he didn't, then let Him kill me.

Where does our confidence go in the face of trials and the storms of life? How does our boat rock when the waves of adversity rise and seem ready to engulf us with no visible way out?

Do we hold on to our integrity as these men did? Do we hold on to His promise to be with us *'even to the end of the age'*? (Matthew 28:20). Do we hold on even if He does not deliver us? It is hard, in the face of trials and disappointment, to keep hoping and believing that our breakthrough will come, and we will be victorious. But we must not forget that if God is for us, no one can be against us. He loved us so much that He gave His only begotten son as a sacrifice for our sins. Nothing and no one can separate us from the love of Christ. Even in the face of death, *'we are more than conquerors through Him who loved us. For I am convinced that neither height nor depth, nor anything else in all creation, will be able to separate us from the love of God that is in Christ Jesus our Lord'* (see Romans 8: 31-39 NIV).

God came through for Shadrach, Meshach and Abednego. Their defiance led to their promotion and the proclamation by King Nebuchadnezzar that no other god can save the way God had saved them. The Bible gives several examples of people who came out victorious after holding onto their faith and integrity: Daniel, Job, Paul and Silas, and Peter to mention a few. The Bible also mentions our heroes of faith, some of whom did not receive the things they were promised before they died. Did that make them lose faith? No. Did that make God less God? Absolutely not! These people knew they were only foreigners and strangers here on this earth. They had their eyes on something better and grander than all this world could offer. They had their eyes on the hope and joy of living eternally with our LORD in heaven. They saw the bigger picture with their eyes of faith. When we tap into the realm of faith, we see things that human eyes cannot see and have knowledge that others cannot fathom. We can stand tall and unfazed in the face of adversity because we know Whom we have believed and that He is able to hold that which we have committed unto Him until that day when we see Him face-to-face (2 Timothy 1:12). By having this attitude, we make God proud of us as His heirs. We make the sacrifice of God's Son worth it because we are worthy of His love.

Chapter SEVEN

GOD'S MASTER PLAN

'Sisi, please call me biko.'[1] That was the message I got from Temi on the 3rd of December 2016. She had just arrived in India a few days before for a follow-up visit and was still slightly jet-lagged. The plan was to have her routine tests and scans done and see the oncologist. It was meant to be a short visit and she planned to probably spend Christmas there and then head back home. It was not meant to be a complicated trip… at least, that was the plan.

> *'Many plans are in a man's mind, but it is the Lord's purpose for him that will stand.' (Proverbs 19:21 AMPC)*

Our lives are filled with and ruled by plans, planning and yet more plans. We plan to get a degree, get married, have children, travel the world, build a house, buy a car, go on holiday, meet a friend; the list is endless. However, how many of those plans are truly flexible and how do we cope when our plans are interrupted or changed? The truth is that many of us make plans but forget to get the Master Planner involved, so when He decides to change those plans to fit in with His will, we are not prepared.

> *'"For I know the plans I have for you," declares the Lord, "plans to prosper you and not to harm you, plans to give you hope and a future."' (Jeremiah 29:11 NIV)*

God has plans to give us hope and a future either for this life or in eternity with Him when He calls us home. How flexible we are in yielding to His will and plans will determine our response when things do not go our way.

---

[1]*'Biko' is an Igbo word meaning 'please'.*

Temi's prognosis was poor. The cancer had returned very soon after initial treatment and had metastasised to her liver and bones. The doctors had had high hopes for her but were disappointed when the treatment failed. She had been counted as one of their success stories. She had been interviewed and this had been recorded on the website in promotion of their hospital as a successful cancer treatment centre. Now they were thinking of second-line treatment. The options were laid out for us, with so much to think about. Chemotherapy again and all that comes with it. This was not how Temi had thought the year would end. This was not what we had planned for this year. It was December and Christmas was fast approaching. Here she was again, in a foreign land, far from home and family, facing disease and more treatment.

It would have been so easy to lose hope and feel overwhelmed with the events of the past few weeks. But Temi remained hopeful. We all did. There was nothing God could not do, and we held onto His words and His promises. Like the prophet Jeremiah, Temi's prayer was:

> 'Heal me, O Lord, and I shall be healed; Save me, and I shall be saved, For You are my praise... Let them be ashamed who persecute me, but do not let me be put to shame; Let them be dismayed, but do not let me be dismayed. Bring on them the day of doom, And destroy them with double destruction!' (Jeremiah 17:14,18 NKJV)

God knew what He was doing. God knew the cancer would recur. He knew it would spread to her liver and bones and then her lungs. He knew all this because nothing catches Him unawares. Now, one may ask, if He knew all this, why did He allow it to happen? Why did she have to suffer so? Why did He not heal her completely? The answer is that God does not share His glory with any other. He sees the whole picture. He works all things out for our good and His glory. Our whole life is laid out before Him and He knows how our story will end.

> *'For you created my inmost being; you knit me together in my mother's womb… My frame was not hidden from you when I was made in the secret place, when I was woven together in the depths of the earth. Your eyes saw my unformed body; all the days ordained for me were written in your book before one of them came to be. How precious to me are your thoughts, God! How vast is the sum of them!' (Psalm 139: 13, 15-17 NIV)*

It is such an amazing thought that even before one of our days came to be, God had already charted our course. He knew what our history would look like. As humans, we have grand plans, and our lives are filled with struggles to achieve those plans. We strive and keep going until we reach that level that we had envisaged from the start. Nobody plans to get derailed or taken off course; we just do not normally plan for such eventualities. The fact is that we do not see the whole picture. If we could take a look from God's point of view, then things would not take us by surprise or catch us off guard. God knows we are weak and prone to making wrong decisions, so even if we make plans, they might not be what God wanted for us. God has a way of re-directing our steps so that we fall in line with what He'd originally planned for us. He has a way of knocking the props from beneath us so we can learn to depend on Him. That also applies to the plans we make for ourselves. We need to learn to put God in charge of every aspect of our lives, learn to live by His blueprints and then we will see things work out better for us.

> *'Roll your works upon the Lord [commit and trust them wholly to Him; He will cause your thoughts to become agreeable to His will, and] so shall your plans be established and succeed.' (Proverbs 16:3 AMPC)*

So, what plans have we made for tomorrow? What have we got lined up for the week, or the month or even the next few years of our lives? Was God involved in our planning, or did we leave Him out of it altogether? Many times, we do not remember to bring God into our situation until we have hit an iceberg. Then we suddenly remember to call on Him. God does not want to be a last resort. He wants to be the first port of call. He wants to be on the planning committee with us. He desires to be involved in every aspect of our lives because He loves us and wants everything to work out for us according to His will. We would save ourselves from many a heartache if we would just get Him involved from the beginning.

> *'Within your heart you can make plans for your future, but the Lord chooses the steps you take to get there.' (Proverbs 16:9 TPT)*

> *'Remember the former things, those of long ago; I am God, and there is no other; I am God, and there is none like me. I make known the end from the beginning, from ancient times, what is still to come. I say, "My purpose will stand, and I will do all that I please."' (Isaiah 46:9-10 NIV)*

Chapter EIGHT

UNCONDITIONAL LOVE

*'The Lord appeared to us in the past, saying:
"I have loved you with an everlasting love;
I have drawn you with unfailing kindness."'
(Jeremiah 31:3 NIV)*

God loves us unconditionally with a never-ending love. Even when we drift far away from Him, He remains faithful, waiting for us to come back to Him, and He does not cast us away. He takes us back, no matter how broken we have become, all because He loves us. Sometimes, we wonder… if He loves us so, why doesn't He spare us from pain? Why doesn't He make it all go away? He loved Jesus so much, yet allowed Him to go through pain and rejection. All He went through was for our redemption, to bring us back to Himself so that no matter what we face, we would never be without His love.

I called the doctor in India, just to have a better picture of what was going on. Temi had been started on Gemcitabine, a second-line chemotherapy regime, but she seemed to be having many complications, from low white blood cell count to low haemoglobin level plus fluid in her lungs. She had to have a tube inserted to drain the fluid so she could breathe and have some relief from the pain she was in. She was on strong painkillers but at times the pain was so much. The way things were going, it did not look as though the chemotherapy regime was working.

The intravenous chemotherapy was stopped and changed to Capecitabine, which was oral. Things seemed to settle down a bit and then she developed terrible waist pain and hand and foot syndrome, which was very uncomfortable. It seemed as if her system was gradually shutting down. There was a suggestion that she could interrupt treatment to see if she had any relief from the horrible side effects. Then one day, I received a message from Temi's doctor: 'Temi showed up today after eight days in Emergency with breathlessness. She has disseminated disease, spread to lungs, liver and bones. We are now left with limited treatment options. It may be better for her to travel back to Nigeria with a treatment schedule proposed from here, and be with and near dear ones.' That's when it hit me; there was nothing more they could do. They had exhausted all the treatment options and she was getting worse.

What do you do when the doctor says there's nothing more they can do for you? Do you give up? Do you despair? Do you sink into the pit of depression? Or do you look up to God? Temi loved the Lord, but He loved her more. She went through so much pain; she went through so much suffering. But through it all, she remained strong and at peace within herself, so much so that she told me, 'If God will not heal me, then let Him kill me.' When she told me this, I knew that she had a love for Him and He loved her too—this was A LOVE WORTH HAVING. She knew that the God she served had the power to heal her in the way He alone could. Jesus told His disciples:

> *'I have told you these things, so that in Me you may have [perfect] peace and confidence. In the world you have tribulation and trials and distress and frustration; but be of good cheer [take courage; be confident, certain, undaunted]! For I have overcome the world [I have deprived it of power to harm you and have conquered it for you].' (John 16:33 AMPC)*

Being God's children does not mean that we will be spared from pain or hardship. It means that no matter what comes our way, we have His peace. The world finds this hard to understand. We can stay strong through the storm because our eyes are not on the waves but on Him who can calm the storm, on Him who takes hold of our hand, so we will not sink. He is with us in the midst of the storm. He has indeed overcome the world. He gives us a testimony where the world has but a story because even in the eye of the storm, He remains in full control. Can we trust Him to lead us safely through? Can we trust that He knows what He is doing and no matter what the outcome is, He works all things together for our good? When we are in the storm, it is difficult to see any good with our human eyes but when we have come through the storm and look back, we can see how God helped us through. We can see how He was building in us all the while the strength, courage and character that we would not have possessed if He'd kept us from the storm.

Temi remained a source of encouragement to others, even though she was in pain. She went to see a friend who was also battling cancer and encouraged him, even on his deathbed. She felt sad when she heard of the passing away of anyone she had been in contact with who was fighting cancer. She had a beautiful spirit that made others want to know her and be her friend, and she always had a word of encouragement, even for me, her eldest sister, as I fought my own cancer battle. She taught me strength and courage in the face of adversity. We shared laughs and moments of sadness too, even though we were thousands of miles apart.

Coming back to Nigeria was a miracle on its own for her. Preparations were being made for the management of the disease and control of her symptoms. She still had the tube inserted to drain the fluid in her lungs. She needed a 'Fit to fly' certificate to enable her to fly back home. And she needed pain relief—lots of it. Our earnest prayer was that she would make it back home in time. We could not imagine her dying in a foreign land, away from family. That would have been unbearable for all of us. We prayed and God answered. A few days before her flight, she went back to the hospital for an X-ray so they could drain as much fluid as they could to make her comfortable. The tube had to be removed as it would have been difficult to get a 'Fit to fly' certificate and fly with the tube still in situ. She was given strong pain killers to travel with and finally, she arrived in Nigeria.

At last, Temi was home, amongst family, with those she loved and who loved her dearly. God had ordained that during that period, my family and I would be visiting Nigeria. He knew what He was doing. He planned everything to the last detail. I got to spend time with her during her last few days on earth, and I cherish those moments. During that time, we had support from friends and brothers and sisters in Christ who visited and prayed with us. She had doctors come to visit her at home and provide prescriptions for palliative medications to keep her comfortable. Our brief holiday in Nigeria came to an end and my family and I had to travel back home to the UK. It was the hardest thing I have ever had to do. I wished I could stay with her but I just had to trust that God had everything covered. She was His daughter after all and He loved her dearly. I told her that she was in the able hands of our Lord who neither sleeps nor slumbers.

Two days after we left Nigeria, Temi's pain became worse. I spoke to her over the phone and encouraged her to take the pain relief medication that had been prescribed for her, and not try to endure the pain. When her symptoms worsened, she had to be admitted to the hospital. She was in the intensive care unit. Again, God granted favour and she had a supportive medical team around her.

It was Friday the 15th of September. Temi had been in hospital for almost three weeks but was out of the intensive care unit. She was unable to eat and barely conscious by this time. Thankfully, her pain was under control. I had been getting daily updates from Dad on her condition. Anu, who had by this time gone back to Abuja because she had been off work caring for Temi, was restless. She felt she needed return to Jos so she set off shortly after midday. I was at work that day as usual. I was also restless. A patient on the ward I was working on had just died and I did something I'd never done before—I cried. Why did the patient's death affect me so? Maybe because there were several similarities between her case and Temi's case, or maybe God was just preparing me for what was ahead.

It was almost 5 pm. Anu arrived in Jos and went straight to the hospital. As soon as she got there, and Dad saw her, he knew it was time for him to head home. He didn't scold her for coming back so soon after she'd left Jos. He just felt it was the right thing at the right time.

Shortly after 6 pm, I sent Dad a text message with this Bible verse:

> 'We are hard pressed on every side, but not crushed; perplexed, but not in despair; persecuted, but not abandoned; struck down, but not destroyed.' (2 Corinthians 4:8-9 NIVUK)

His words to me were, 'Couldn't be more true than now. I cannot think of a time more stressful for me in recent time than what we are going through right now. May the good Lord help us through.' All I could say in reply was, 'Amen. It is well, Dad. It is well.'

I was waiting on Anu to give me updates on how Temi was doing. I was still restless but somehow felt better that Anu was with her. I wished I could be there too and Anu wished the same. Temi's breathing had become laboured. Anu confessed that she was not looking so well. The doctor on call was thinking of moving her back to the intensive care unit because he was not comfortable with the way she was breathing. She was put on oxygen.

Shortly before 10 pm, I felt the urge to see her so I asked Anu if I could do a video call. I did not intend to say anything because by this time she could not speak, also there was another patient in the room. I just wanted to see her again. Initially, Anu was reluctant but then she acquiesced. When I saw her, I felt that the time was near and her struggles would soon be over. I saw her and was overwhelmed with so much love for the brave warrior that she was. I ended the call but told Anu to whisper in her ear that it was okay to let go. This was my final act of surrender.

I could not sleep. I felt so overwhelmed that Anu was bearing this burden alone. I could only pray as I listened to a praise and worship playlist by Hillsong. At 12:36 am, I got a text message from a dear sister in my church here in the UK. She had been praying along with us for Temi. It read: 'Just in case you're still awake and praying, I am joining you... Temi is in His hands: What better place to be... He knows her suffering and yours. I sense it is hard to give it to Him. Lord, in your eternal mercy, lighten Temi's burden and suffering as well as her family's. Amen. xxx.'

I tried to reach Anu again. She did not respond to my text asking how Temi was. Then shortly after 1:00 am, she sent a text asking for Dr Ushie's number. I sent it to her but she still did not tell me what was happening. I was now getting frantic. It was over an hour later when she responded and I asked again, 'How is she?'

Her reply turned my world upside down: 'Our baby earned her angel wings by 12:22 am this morning. She didn't struggle. She was in my arms.'

I was broken. We all were.

Temi went to be with the Lord on the 16th of September 2017, shortly after midnight, four days before her thirty-third birthday. She was at peace because the Lord gave her peace. She was a courageous warrior who'd fought with all she had, knowing God was with her. He took her home because He knew that was best for her. It was, and still is painful to us, her family and all who loved her. We miss her and wish she were still here with us, but God ultimately does get the glory. He healed her in His own way, setting her free from the chains of cancer forever. Her mortal body was laid to rest on her birthday.

As God's children, we pray and ask God for healing or blessing or breakthrough. Sometimes we get the answers we want, but other times we do not. Instead, God gives us what we need, so that He might be glorified. When that happens, it is not time for us to be bitter towards God. Instead, we should ask Him to show us what He is helping us to become by letting us go through such pain. In time, He lets us see how much we overcame and how far He has led us from where we first began. In time, His plans for us will unfold, as He leads us to that place where we will know no sorrow or pain or shame.

> *'And I heard a loud voice from the throne saying, "Look! God's dwelling place is now among the people, and He will dwell with them. They will be His people, and God Himself will be with them and be their God. 'He will wipe every tear from their eyes. There will be no more death or mourning or crying or pain, for the old order of things has passed away.'" (Revelation 21:3-4 NIV)*

Chapter Nine

FINISHING STRONG

I remember when Temi first told me she had started writing about her cancer journey. I felt so proud of her. She said she'd always wanted to write but never had a reason to before. She had kept a journal so writing came a bit easier for her. At least she was bold enough to begin, which was more than I could say for myself. During the period I was on admission in hospital after my surgery, I had felt strongly within me that I should be writing, in fact, a few people who came to visit me said I needed to write about my experience. But the truth was, I just didn't know how to begin. Call it 'writer's block' or whatever you think, I had the words in my head, but to put them down was just so hard. I shared with Temi that I felt I needed to write too and even had a title for my book. She was so excited and said it sounded really good. 'It's all part of Kingdom growth,' she said. 'If we can touch lives with our stories, we draw people to God and that's our main purpose on earth. Tell the story!' Somehow, I felt we could write the book together and I shared this idea with her. She could continue her writing and I could start mine and somehow, we would find a way to weave our stories together. This sounded like a plan.

So, I started. I managed to write a bit of an introduction but the words were just not flowing. I got stuck. I just could not get my hands to type the words I had in my head. It wasn't for lack of anything to share, because I had a lot to share. Having had three surgeries and spending three and a half months in hospital with a traumatic recovery process, then enduring six cycles of chemotherapy, I surely had a story to tell. But I just could not write. So, I put it all on hold until I felt it was the right time but Temi kept writing. She wrote until her condition worsened and she was unable to write any longer. Despite her failing health, she still encouraged me to write and I know she would have wanted to complete this book because she had a story to tell.

Eight days after Temi died, Daddy sent me her manuscript to read. She had only gotten as far as the beginning of Chapter Six. I must confess that at this time, the pain of losing her was still very raw so I could not bring myself to read it as I knew it would be very emotional. But I knew what I needed to do; I needed to finish her story! However, I didn't have the courage to even read what she had written, so how could I possibly pick up from where she'd stopped? I needed to know how the next piece of the puzzle fitted in. I even asked my siblings to read the manuscript and see if there was anything they felt they needed to add to the story but I suppose this was just my desperate attempt to postpone the inevitable. I did what I knew best at the time, I put it on hold and told Daddy that I would begin working on the book after I'd finished reading it. I had my diploma exams coming up during the first quarter of 2018 so my focus was on getting through those. And that was it for two whole years. I did not write a word!

I successfully completed my diploma in March 2020 and then I knew I had no more excuses. By this time, I had read the manuscript. Slowly but surely, I began to write. I set myself a deadline. I wanted to finish by the third anniversary of her death in September. This was good for me as I love working to deadlines. There were a few times I had to refer to text messages from Temi or posts she'd made on a few social media platforms to fill in gaps.

As I continued to write, the words continued to flow. At last, I had got into the rhythm of things! Sometimes I felt like Temi was whispering to me as I wrote. She had such a profound impact on my life and encouraged me not to give up. I remember the last conversation I had with her before we left Nigeria, less than three weeks before her death. Somehow, it was as if she'd known that would be the last time we would see each other in person. The last thing she told me as I kissed her goodbye was 'Be a man.' I knew what she meant. She needed me to be strong, not just for myself, but for my dad and my siblings. So, even though I had my own battles to fight, I still needed to be strong.

I fought so hard to keep the tears back. I promised myself that I would be strong. I knew I could not do this on my own, and one verse from scripture kept recurring at various times during the year:

> *'So do not fear, for I am with you; do not be dismayed, for I am your God. I will strengthen you and help you; I will uphold you with my righteous right hand. (Isaiah 41:10 NIV)*

This was God's reminder and confirmation that He was in this with me. I had nothing to fear because I would finish Temi's story.

As I continued to write, I felt something else. Just like Temi had said when she'd asked God for His revelation to her concerning her diagnosis, God reminded me of the same verse in John chapter 11:

> *'When Jesus heard that, he said "This sickness is not unto death, but for the glory of God, that the Son of God may be glorified through it."' (NKJV)*

Temi's story was not going to end in her death. I felt that God wanted to use her story to encourage and help other people who might be in a similar situation. And I was going to finish what she started.

Being in the United Kingdom at the time of my diagnosis with ovarian cancer in October 2015 meant that due to my age, my oncologist automatically referred me for genetic testing. Having had family history of cancer—first my mum, then Temi and me—my oncologist felt it was likely genetic. Before this time, we had not connected my mum's diagnosis with the occurrence of breast cancer in Temi and me having ovarian cancer, as her diagnosis was not really clear. She had been diagnosed with lung adenocarcinoma in Nigeria and we just did not understand how this was possible especially as she did not have any pre-disposing risk factors. However, when I told my oncologist this, she was of the opinion it was likely related to ovarian cancer which is why she encouraged me to have the genetics test.

I had the test done in February 2016, shortly before I started chemotherapy and I received the results in the middle of April 2016. I found out that I had the BRCA1 genetic mutation which puts one at risk of both breast and ovarian cancer. I was given a letter to send to my siblings informing them of the results of the genetic test and providing information on how they could access the test if they decided to do so. I sent a copy of the letter to Temi - who was already in India by this time - and encouraged her to ask her doctor if she could do the test too. Temi's doctor in India had said that there was no need for her to get tested because she already had breast cancer, and going by my diagnosis, it was very likely she had the genetic mutation too. The result of my test made Mum's diagnosis look less likely what the doctors had told us and more likely a BRCA-related cancer. Before now, I had never heard of the BRCA gene mutation. Maybe if we'd heard of it at the time our mum had died, and if we had been certain of what her diagnosis was, then it would have been considered. We might not have been able to change any outcome but we would have been better informed.

Genetics testing is not routinely offered to patients in Nigeria who have had breast or ovarian cancer or to their family members. This has led to cases of breast and ovarian cancer in women with strong family histories. Symptoms of ovarian cancer are not easily recognised and some women have even been misdiagnosed. This has led to diagnosis at later stages when survival is greatly reduced due to the extent of disease. God has blessed mankind with technology that can help reduce this risk after appropriate counselling and thus reduce the incidence of breast and ovarian cancer and/or improve the survival rate amongst those with the BRCA gene mutation. Unfortunately, many women in Nigeria are still dying and this really breaks my heart. If only there was increased awareness of this genetic mutation... If only genetic testing was routinely available and affordable in Nigeria for those with a strong family history of breast and or ovarian cancer... If only people were more self-aware of what is normal and what is abnormal and would not ignore their symptoms... If only the healthcare system in Nigeria could make cancer diagnosis and treatment a priority and make things available at affordable costs within Nigeria so that people would not have to seek expensive treatment abroad... If only people with cancer symptoms could be taken seriously and not misdiagnosed... then maybe many more women and men could survive these cancers.

My hope and vision for the future is that more awareness would be raised around the BRCA gene mutation and the risk it carries for both breast and ovarian cancer. It is my hope that genetic testing would be made available in Nigeria for those with a family history of breast and ovarian cancer so that many more women would be able to make an informed choice for preventative measures. This could lead to early diagnosis and give women a greater chance of survival.

Temi was diligent in her self-examination and that was how she noticed the lump. She did not accept the first doctor's report who told her all was well when she did not feel well. I did not feel well in myself and even after my symptoms had been dismissed by several doctors. I was constipated and felt bloated, I had pain in my abdomen and I could feel a lump. I kept going back until decisive action was taken that led to my diagnosis. We both prayed about our symptoms, but we did not take anything for granted.

In an Instagram post on the 30th of October 2016, shortly after the completion of her initial treatment and radiotherapy, and in recognition of Breast Cancer Awareness month, Temi had this to say: 'The trauma, the pain, the battle, the low blood counts, the side effects, the scars, hair loss, hormonal change, emotional stress, tears, insomnia, amnesia, breathlessness, loss of appetite, nausea, lymphoedema, numbness, dead taste buds ... It really is a lot to have to deal with. Don't wait. Don't assume.

You can avoid the trauma that comes with cancer treatment; surgery, chemotherapy, radiation. You can avoid the fight, the struggle for life. Get checked! Do your breast self-examination. Book an appointment with your GP. Have a mammogram done, know your body. Early detection really saves. Tell your sister and your wife or your girlfriend to tell their sisters, friends and their friends that early detection is the best form of protection. Don't wait or assume. Let me be the one with the scars while you be the one to get checked! No woman deserves to die from breast cancer. Spread the word. Better to mammogram your boobs than Instagram them. #thepinkmonth is ending but the awareness doesn't end.'

We were persistent in seeking solutions. Sometimes, persistence is the key to receiving your breakthrough. The persistent widow was granted justice against her adversary because she did not give up. Jesus used this as an illustration to emphasise the point that we should always pray and not give up (Luke 18:1-5).

Have you knocked at several doors and none has opened up for you? Keep knocking.

Have you called out for so long and no help has come? Keep calling out.

Have you given up on your God-given dream? Keep working on it.

Have you prayed and not yet received an answer? Keep praying.

I encourage you to remain steadfast. You have come too far to let it all go to waste. The race is almost over. The finish line is just over the horizon. Just a few more steps and the prize will be yours. It might be difficult to take those last steps after such a long and arduous journey. It might be easier to throw in the towel. But the Lord is at the finish line, waiting to welcome His faithful servants home. Keep your eyes on Him and keep your eyes on the prize. He is there to welcome you home.

'His master replied, "Well done, good and faithful servant! You have been faithful with a few things; I will put you in charge of many things. Come and share your master's happiness!"' (Matthew 25:21 NIV)

And like Paul wrote to Timothy towards the end of his time on earth, we can say:

'I have fought the good fight, I have finished the race, I have kept the faith. Now there is in store for me the crown of righteousness, which the Lord, the righteous Judge, will award to me on that day—and not only to me, but also to all who have longed for his appearing.' (2 Timothy 4:7-8 NIV)

For those still fighting one battle or the other, here are a few last words from Temi to encourage you:

'Thank God we don't look like what we are going through or what we have been through.'

'Thanks be to God who always leads us in triumph in Christ, and through us diffuses the fragrance of His knowledge in every place. For we are to God the fragrance of Christ among those who are being saved and among those who are perishing.' (2 Corinthians 2:14-15 NKJV)

'No matter how hard things get, always find a reason or reasons to smile. Also, always remember things to be thankful for. Today and always I'm thankful for life. You never know the value of it until you almost lose it.'

'#God all the way! #BreastCancerSurvivor #CancerSucks #CancerReallySucks #Survivor #Strength #Hope #Courage #Fighter #WithGodICan #Metastasis in my liver and bone BUT #MyGodIsBiggerThanCancer.'

Temilolu Adegboye
(20th September 1984—16th September 2017)

PICTURE GALLERY

TEMI AND ANU BEFORE BIOPSY IN NIGERIA

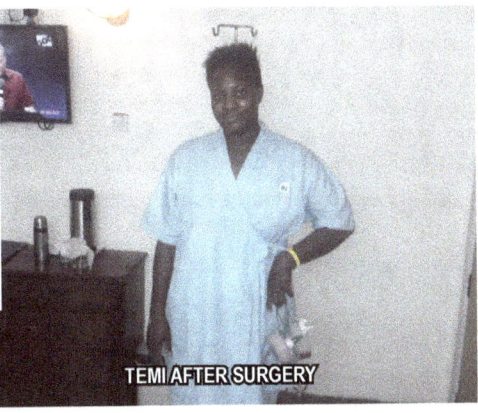
TEMI AFTER SURGERY

TEMI AFTER SURGERY

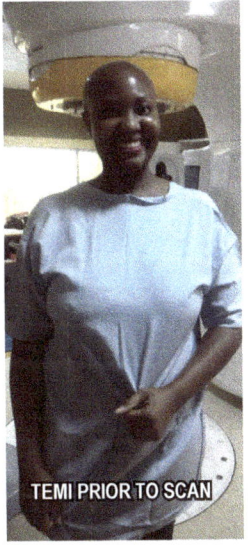
TEMI PRIOR TO SCAN

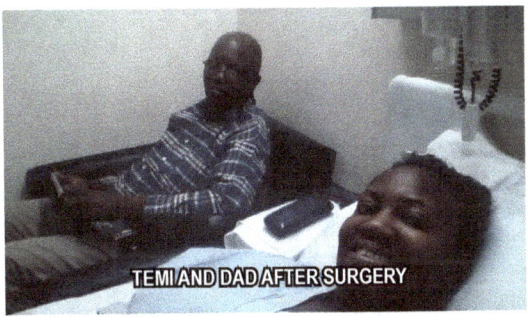
TEMI AFTER SURGERY

TEMI AND DAD AFTER SURGERY

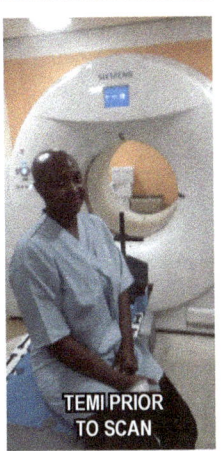
TEMI PRIOR TO SCAN

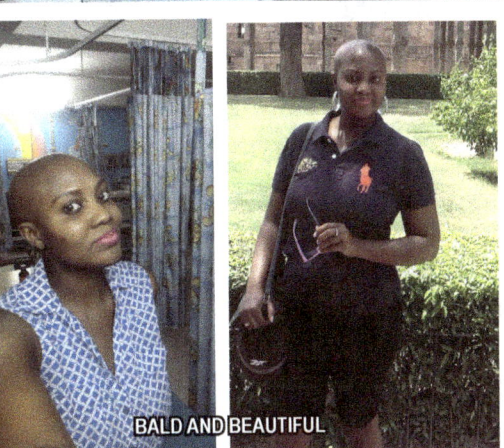
BALD AND BEAUTIFUL

TEMI WEARING A WIG

A LOVE WORTH HAVING

CANCER AWARENESS

TEMI

TEMI

TEMI DOWN BUT NOT OUT

TEMI AND ANU

TEMI AND ANU

CANCER AWARENESS WALK - TEMI AND ANU

CANCER AWARENESS- TEMI AND ANU

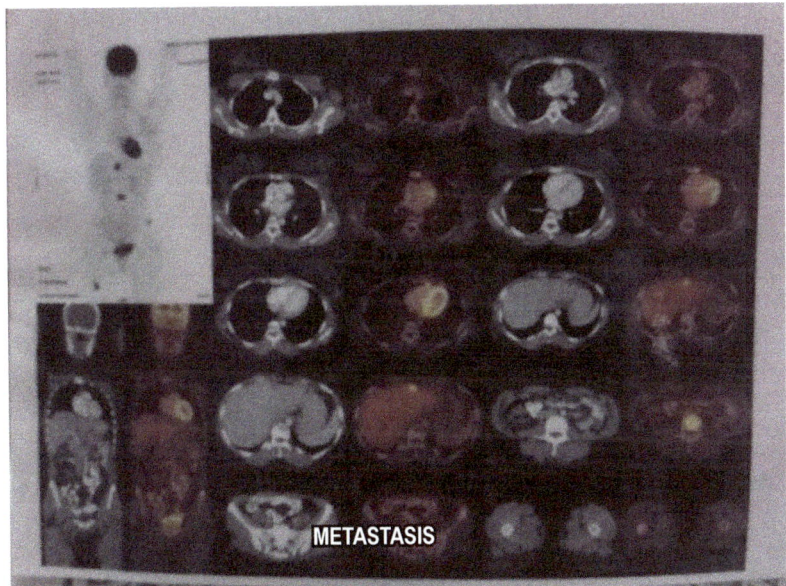
METASTASIS

TEMI, ANU, ISAAC, MAMA

ANU, TEMI AND SUSANNAH

Further Information:

If you, your family or friends have any questions or concerns about breast and/or ovarian cancer and the genetic risks, you can visit the following websites/links for further information:

https://breastcancernow.org/

https://www.cancerresearchuk.org/about-cancer/breast-cancer

https://www.cancerresearchuk.org/about-cancer/ovarian-cancer

https://www.macmillan.org.uk/

https://www.macmillan.org.uk/cancer-information-and-support/worried-about-cancer/causes-and-risk-factors/brca-gene

https://www.ovacome.org.uk/

https://ovarian.org.uk/

https://targetovariancancer.org.uk/

https://targetovariancancer.org.uk/about-ovarian-cancer/hereditary-ovarian-cancer/getting-tested

ABOUT THE AUTHORS

Temilolu Adegboye, popularly called 'Temi' by those who knew her, was a vibrant young woman who was loved by everyone. She was the fourth child born to Rev. David Adegboye and Late Mrs Oluyinka Adegboye in Jos, Nigeria on the 20th September 1984. She loved the Lord and held firmly to her faith in Him. She studied Cinematography at the National Film Institute (NFI), Jos, Nigeria and lived and worked in Abuja, Nigeria. She was, until her death on the 16th September 2017, an avid campaigner for breast cancer awareness. She took part in breast cancer awareness events in Nigeria. She is survived by Dad, Rev. David Adegboye, Stepmum, Mrs Felicia Adegboye, siblings Susannah Oziegbe (sister), Banke Odujinrin (sister), Wale Adegboye (brother), Anu Koshemani (sister) and Isaac Adegboye (brother), and nieces and nephews.

For more information, visit: www.temiloluadegboye.com

Susannah Yetunde Oziegbe is a wife and mother and an ovarian cancer survivor. She lives with her husband Daniel and their two children in London, UK. She is the first born of her parents Rev. David Adegboye and Late Mrs Oluyinka Adegboye. She is a Pharmacist.

She became a Christian at the young age of five and has seen her walk with God grow over the years.

She sings as part of the worship team and is one of the children's leaders in The BEAR Church, London. She loves reading and writing and is working on her solo book projects. She supports the work of several charities for women diagnosed with breast and ovarian cancer. She hopes to start a Foundation in memory of her late sister Temilolu Adegboye, to help support the early diagnosis of breast and ovarian cancer due to the BRCA gene mutation in Nigerian women.

Read more about Susannah's story at: www.targetovariancancer.org.uk/stories/susannahs-story

Connect with Susannah to see what God is doing in her life and through her:

Website: www.sueyetzie.com

Instagram: @sueyetzie

Facebook: Susannah Yetunde Oziegbe

Twitter: @syetzie

www.ingramcontent.com/pod-product-compliance
Lightning Source LLC
Chambersburg PA
CBHW050440010526
44118CB00013B/1611